VEGETABLES ON FIRE

VEGETABLES ON FIRE

50 Vegetable-Centered
Meals from the Grill

BROOKE LEWY

Photographs by
Erin Kunkel

CHRONICLE BOOKS
SAN FRANCISCO

Library of Congress Cataloging-in-Publication Data

Names: Lewy, Brooke, author. | Kunkel, Erin, photographer.
Title: Vegetables on fire : 50 vegetable-centered meals from the
   grill / by Brooke Lewy ; photographs by Erin Kunkel.
Description: San Francisco : Chronicle Books, [2017] | Includes index.
Identifiers: LCCN 2016039241 | ISBN 9781452158242 (hardcover : alk. paper)
Subjects: LCSH: Barbecuing. | Cooking (Vegetables) | LCGFT: Cookbooks.
Classification: LCC TX840.B3 L4615 2017 | DDC 641.6/5—dc23 LC record available at
https://lccn.loc.gov/2016039241

Manufactured in China

Photographs by Erin Kunkel
Food styling by Lillian Kang
Prop styling by Claire Mack

Designed by Alice Chau

10 9 8 7 6 5 4 3 2 1

Chronicle books and gifts are available at special quantity discounts to corporations, professional
associations, literacy programs, and other organizations. For details and discount information, please
contact our premiums department at corporatesales@chroniclebooks.com or at 1-800-759-0190.

Chronicle Books LLC
680 Second Street
San Francisco, California 94107
www.chroniclebooks.com

For Scott and Sammy

CONTENTS

INTRODUCTION

There's a promise that goes along with grilling—sunshine, fresh air, yellow mustard, ice-cold beers. Friends gather around and toast the cook as he or she loads the table with piles of saucy chicken and snappy hot dogs. And then, usually on the side, slices of eggplant and zucchini wanly line a plate. Those vegetables are limp, and maybe a little slippery. They're not intentionally bland; it was just that no one really thought about them.

Here's the thing: grilled vegetables don't have to be uninspired. Whether you're a vegetarian or just someone who's crowding more vegetables onto your plate, here's a little nudging to give produce its time on the grill. For whatever reason—personal health, skepticism toward conventional cattle farming, a tight budget, a killer farmers' market nearby—a vegetable-centric way of eating is becoming the norm for so many, and it can absolutely move outside to become part of your summer grilling fare. The following pages marry great vegetables, the grill, and a lot of supporting flavors—tahini, tons of fresh herbs, miso, tangy vinegars—to create dozens of delicious, satisfying meals that stand on their own.

And here's the other thing: grilling should be casual. It should be done with a glass of rosé in hand, some good tunes, and friends who feel like family. The recipes in this book embrace that summer vibe. They're not fussy, and many of the parts and pieces can be made ahead of time. They recognize that every grill is different, and they acknowledge that, yes, sometimes what you really need is a delicious chimichurri to go with that simply grilled eggplant. They understand that if you're grilling, you definitely don't want to turn on the oven (and maybe not even the stove), and you certainly want to wash as few dishes as possible. (Remember that glass of rosé?) We all know that some of the best things about grilling, aside from that smoky, crisp-edged flavor, are that your house stays cool and you don't have pots and pans to scrub when everyone goes home.

Grilling vegetables inherently makes them a little softer and sweeter, and of course, smoky. What all of these veggies, from bright carrots to halved heads of romaine, want to round them out is salt; something with a little fat, like miso butter, feta, or lemon aioli; and some crunch, like toasted nuts or golden croutons. Every recipe here creates that satisfying balance and stands as a lunch or dinner on its own. Go ahead: put these vegetables at the center of your grill; they can take it.

TECHNIQUES, TIPS, AND EQUIPMENT

KNIFE WORK

Whether your vegetables are from the grocery store or your local farmers' market, cutting them to the proper shape is important, since, for the most part, you want them to cook evenly. Generally, grilling vegetables means short cooking times, and a little more care in the knife work can mean the difference between delightfully crisp-tender vegetables and vegetables that are blackened on the outside and raw on the inside. A good, sharp knife makes cutting and slicing the vegetables a more pleasant process.

ABOUT OIL AND SALT

Some recipes call for olive oil, some for vegetable oil, such as canola. For coating the vegetables before grilling, both oils work just fine. The recipes aim for consistency, so you don't have to have two oils cluttering your kitchen counter at the same time. For dishes where the oil is included in a dressing or used in a way other than coating produce before grilling, be sure to use the one called for and the amount specified, as it will affect the flavor. In almost every recipe, the vegetables need to be coated in oil before finding their way to the grill. This not only adds flavor and prevents sticking, but it keeps them from drying out. The amount of oil necessary is approximate; you just need enough to lightly coat the whole vegetable.

This book uses two kinds of salt: one for cooking and one for finishing. Nearly all of the salt called for is kosher salt. It's kosher salt that we use to season before any of the veggies hit the dips. The other salt called for is finishing salt. Kosher salt first: the recipes here were developed and tested with Diamond Crystal brand kosher salt, which is less dense and salty than both Morton brand kosher salt and table salt. If you're cooking with either of the two latter types, cut the salt in half and use a light hand when sprinkling your pre-grilled vegetables; you can always add more later. Like coating your vegetables with oil, seasoning them before they hit the grill is important. Amounts are approximate; a pinch is about ⅛ teaspoon. Hold your hand high—a foot above the food—and sprinkle salt in a light, even layer. Now, finishing salt: several of the dishes in this book also call for finishing salt, like Maldon Sea Salt, which has larger, softer flakes, to be added as a final step before serving for a last hit of flavor and some nice, gentle crunch.

EQUIPMENT

Get to know your grill. If you're using a charcoal grill, try skipping the lighter fluid and using a chimney. Pile your charcoal in the top, light two or three crumpled sheets of newspaper in the bottom, and let the packed chimney sit for 10 minutes on the bottom grill rack until the coals are glowing orange. Next, carefully dump the coals onto the lower rack of the grill and replace the top rack. Let the top rack heat for 5 minutes or so and then scrape the grate clean with a wire brush. Sometimes, oiling your grate is necessary; most often oiling the vegetables is enough to prevent sticking. If you do need to oil the grate, using tongs, dip a rolled-up paper towel or the cut side of half an onion in oil and rub it on the grate. If you're going for a quick char, add the vegetables now; otherwise, which will be most cases, let the coals die down a bit. If you're planning to grill for a while, just after you dump your coals into the grill, add another layer of fresh, unlit coals to the grill on top of the lit layer, and use a grill shovel to mix the lit and unlit coals together a bit. By the time the first batch of coals is spent, the second batch will still be in its prime.

The bonus of a charcoal grill is a more pronounced grilled flavor, a more genuine char, and the ability to make dishes like the Smoked Beets on page 123 truly smoky. The downside is that the fire is a bit harder to control (especially for a dense, large vegetable, such as in the Cauliflower Roast with Anchovy Bread Crumbs, page 56). My advice: practice. Maybe add a few more veggies than you need, at least at the beginning, so you can get a feel for the heat and you're not bummed if some of them get too blackened. If you're using a gas grill, the cooking is more straightforward and forgiving. Make sure to preheat it thoroughly, for at least 10 to 15 minutes on most models. If using a charcoal grill, the majority of your cooking happens with the lid off, so lots of oxygen can get to the coals and keep the fire going. With a gas grill, the cooking is most effective with the grill closed as much as possible, creating a more oven-like environment. This is especially true for something like that Cauliflower Roast with Anchovy Bread Crumbs.

You can determine the heat of your grill in a couple of ways. Many gas grills have external thermometers, you can buy a grill thermometer, or you can also tell by holding your hand over the heat. In general, high heat means 450°F to 650°F [230°C to 340°C], and you should be able to hold your hand about 6 in [15 cm] above the heat for 2 to 3 seconds before you have to move it away. Medium-high is roughly 350°F to 450°F [180°C to 230°C], and you should be

able to hold your hand over the coals for 4 to 6 seconds. Medium is about 325°F to 375°F [165°C to 190°C], and you should be able to hold your hand steady for 6 to 7 seconds. Lastly, medium-low is around 250°F to 325°F [120°C to 165°C], and 8 to 10 seconds using the hand test.

In general, vegetables can handle quick cooking over a pretty hot fire. Most of the recipes in this book call for cooking in that medium-high range, so that the exteriors caramelize and crisp before the insides become too soft. The main exception is for denser vegetables such as regular potatoes and sweet potatoes, as well as winter squash, which benefit from lower, gentler heat. In most cases, you want to cook your vegetables until they're cooked through, with lovely, even grill marks, slightly charred edges, and golden spots. Times provided are approximate. You'll have to go by visual cues and feel. It may take a couple of tries to learn about your grill's hot and cool spots and how to move the veggies around to cook them properly. Just try your best and be patient. You will be rewarded with new techniques and delicious meals. No more bland, limp zucchini slices.

Someone will look at this book and wonder: "Do I need to have a grill to make these recipes?" Or "What about the wintertime when my grill is buried under snow?" Good news: you can make nearly all of these recipes inside. The vegetables can be broiled or roasted at a high heat (425°F to 450°F/220°C to 230°C) on a baking sheet in the oven, or you can replicate that seared crispness in a grill pan or a cast-iron skillet on the stovetop. Want to know which way to go? In general, if the vegetable needs to be cooked through—think roots and brassicas—go for the oven. If you're looking to quickly sear the exterior of the vegetable, as with any of the leafy greens, use the stovetop method. In short, don't let limited outdoor space or bad weather stop you. Specific instructions for making each dish indoors are included at the end of each recipe. In the very few cases where the indoor methods are missing, seek out another recipe, as the essence of that particular dish doesn't quite translate to the stove or oven.

As for grilling accessories for vegetables, while there are a million products you could buy, you don't need all of them. Here's what you do need:

- **TONGS:** Long, sturdy tongs are best for getting those vegetables on and off the grill. That said, beware the tongs that come in grilling sets—they're often stiff, a little unwieldy, and may mash up your delicate veggies. Go for regular kitchen tongs instead.

- **A BRUSH:** A silicone brush is great for evenly brushing oil onto veggies, flatbreads, and crostini.

- **A MESH GRILL TOPPER OR COOLING RACK:** These handy accessories keep smaller vegetables—such as mushrooms for the Mushroom and Tofu Spring Rolls (page 114), sugar snap peas, and cubed butternut squash—from falling through the grates. Forget those fancy baskets or Teflon-coated flippers; a mesh grill topper costs $5, is often disposable (but can be used several times), and makes your life easier. Look for them at grocery or hardware stores or online. If you don't want to get a grill-specific topper, a regular cooling rack works as well.

- **HEAVY-DUTY ALUMINUM FOIL:** Foil can stand in for a grill topper in many cases. Also, several recipes in the book call for vegetables to be grilled in a foil packet. Heavy-duty aluminum foil makes for a larger work surface, a sturdier packet, and an easier cleanup.

- **A CAST-IRON OR OTHER OVENPROOF SKILLET:** A few of the recipes call for putting a pan right on the grill (Grilled Shakshuka, page 44,

and Eggplant Rollatini, page 59). Just make sure you have one that's entirely heatproof. (I prefer cast iron.) Also, if there's a component of any dish that needs to be made on the stove, unless the grill needs to be closed to simultaneously cook something else, you can pretty much do everything outside.

- **A BLENDER AND/OR FOOD PROCESSOR:** This book includes a lot of sauces and dips, and for the most part, anything that whirs will make these recipes quick and easy to put together.

Lastly, grilling inevitably means a lot of transferring between the kitchen inside and the grill outside unless you have a whole outdoor kitchen setup. (And, if this is the case, can I come over?) You could use a cutting board or bowl for transport, but baking sheets are enormously useful. What restaurants call quarter sheets (9 by 13 in/22 by 33 cm) are a perfect size for this use. The rim keeps veggies from rolling off, they're great for evenly oiling vegetables that don't fit nicely in a bowl (Hello, carrots and asparagus!), and you can even put them right on the grill.

SLATHERS, DIPS, DRIZZLES, AND BASICS

LEMON VINAIGRETTE, FRESH AND GRILLED

This is a simple, classic vinaigrette, and it works with just about anything. Use it to dress arugula to accompany the Burst and Fresh Tomatoes with Halloumi and Basil Oil (page 42) or to pile on flatbread with peaches (page 136), or to give any simply grilled vegetable a subtle brightness.

¼ cup [60 ml] fresh lemon juice
  (from 1 juicy lemon)
2 Tbsp white wine vinegar
1 tsp finely chopped shallot
1 tsp kosher salt
Freshly ground black pepper
½ cup [120 ml] extra-virgin olive oil

In a jar or small bowl, combine the lemon juice, vinegar, shallot, salt, and pepper and stir or shake. Add the oil and shake or stir again. Taste and add more salt or lemon juice as desired.

For a sweeter, more mellow dressing, grill the lemons before juicing them. To do this, cut them in half and cook over medium heat, cut-side down, until the lemons have caramelized and softened, about 4 minutes. Proceed as above.

INDOOR METHOD: Preheat your broiler. Place lemons on a foil-lined baking tray and roast, cut-side up, until they are caramelized and charred in spots.

Both dressings will keep, refrigerated, for 2 weeks.

SESAME APPLE VINAIGRETTE

This vinaigrette is so much more than the sum of its fairly ordinary parts. A restaurant in Oakland, California, called Hopscotch uses it to dress a crunchy salad (romanesco florets, apples, maybe some arugula, and radishes) that accompanies their perfect fried chicken. Shockingly, it's the salad that takes center stage. You can use it to dress any combination of grilled and raw vegetables.

½ cup [120 ml] apple cider vinegar
¼ cup [60 ml] vegetable oil
1 Tbsp toasted sesame oil
1 tsp kosher salt
Freshly ground black pepper

In a jar, combine the vinegar, vegetable oil, sesame oil, salt, and pepper and shake vigorously. This keeps, refrigerated, for up to 2 weeks. Use it to dress any salad that will go along with a rich main course, or with a meal that includes other Asian flavors like Eggplant Steaks with Miso on page 61.

GREEN GODDESS DRESSING

The fact that this dressing is simultaneously fresh and creamy makes it a standout partner for pretty much any grilled (or raw) vegetables . . . or Falafel-Style Veggie Burgers (page 104), or shrimp, or chicken, or you name it, really. It's also a great way to use up any fresh herbs hanging out in your fridge.

1 cup [240 g] plain, full-fat Greek yogurt
½ cup [120 g] mayonnaise
6 green onions, coarsely chopped
1½ cups [about 30 g] coarsely chopped fresh herbs such as basil, flat-leaf parsley, tarragon, mint, or chervil
Juice from 1 lemon, plus more to taste
3 anchovy fillets
2 garlic cloves, coarsely chopped
1 tsp kosher salt, plus more to taste
Freshly ground black pepper

In a blender or food processor, blend the yogurt, mayonnaise, green onions, herbs, lemon juice, anchovies, garlic, salt, and pepper until smooth. Taste and add more lemon juice, salt, or pepper as desired. This dressing will keep, refrigerated, for up to 1 week.

CHIMICHURRI

This bright, herby sauce traditionally pairs with beef, but it's a great marinade for grilled eggplant and a tasty drizzle over grilled cauliflower.

½ cup [120 ml] red wine vinegar
1 tsp kosher salt, plus more as needed
1 garlic clove, finely grated
1 shallot, finely chopped
1 red or green jalapeño chile, minced
¼ cup [10 g] finely chopped fresh cilantro
¼ cup [10 g] finely chopped flat-leaf parsley
2 Tbsp finely chopped fresh oregano
½ cup [120 ml] extra-virgin olive oil

In a small bowl, stir together the vinegar, salt, garlic, shallot, and chile. Let the mixture stand for 5 minutes. Add the herbs and oil and stir again. Taste and add more salt if desired. Use the same day.

CLASSIC BASIL PESTO

The breadth of the term *pesto* gives you permission to throw pretty much anything into this sauce. The classic basil version is delicious, but you can also add kale to bulk it out, skip the pine nuts, or swap them for pumpkin seeds or bread crumbs. (Both are great alternatives for nut allergies.) You can add Parmesan cheese or pecorino romano, and even a hard, aged Gouda works here. It's also a great way to use up leftover herbs, as pesto freezes well.

2 cups [24 g] packed fresh basil leaves
2 garlic cloves, peeled
¼ cup [30 g] pine nuts
⅔ cup [180 ml] extra-virgin olive oil, or more
1 cup [30 g] coarsely grated Parmesan cheese, or more, to taste
Kosher salt
Freshly ground black pepper

In a food processor, combine the basil, garlic, pine nuts, olive oil, and cheese and blend until smooth. Add more oil if necessary to get the mixture going. Season with salt and pepper. Store the pesto in an airtight container, refrigerated, for up to 1 week, or freeze for up to 6 months. Bring to room temperature before using.

STORAGE TIP: You can also freeze pesto in ice cube trays. Use just a little to stir into vegetable soups or drizzle over caprese salad, or use several cubes to dress a heap of pasta.

CLASSIC AIOLI AND VARIATIONS

Making aioli sounds intimidating, and sometimes, when watching it come together, it seems like magic. But it's more doable than you think. Bonus points for making it by hand—but no sweat if you choose to make it in a food processor or blender instead. The resulting sauce or dip is luscious either way and, with a glance at the variation list (opposite), you can see that it can be taken in many flavor directions.

1 egg yolk

1 to 2 Tbsp fresh lemon juice

1 tsp kosher salt, plus more as needed

1 small garlic clove, finely grated, plus more as needed

⅓ cup [80 ml] olive oil

⅓ cup [80 ml] vegetable oil

To make aioli by hand, in a medium bowl, whisk together the egg yolk, 1 Tbsp lemon juice, salt, and garlic. Twist a kitchen towel to form a ring on your work surface and place the bowl in the middle, so the towel acts as anchor and the bowl stays put. Combine the olive and vegetable oils in a measuring cup (or in a squeeze bottle, if you have it). Then while whisking constantly, add oil one drop at a time and then in a thin steady stream, until the mixture starts to thicken and emulsify. If your aioli gets too thick, thin with more lemon juice, or water, a teaspoon at a time, until it's at your desired consistency. Check for seasoning, adding more lemon juice, salt, or garlic as desired.

To make aioli using a food processor or blender, in the bowl of the appliance, combine the egg yolk, 1 Tbsp lemon juice, salt, and garlic. Pulse to combine. With the motor running, drizzle in the olive and vegetable oils until the aioli is thick and creamy. If your aioli gets too thick, thin with more lemon juice, or water, a teaspoon at a time, until it's at your desired consistency. Check for seasoning, adding more lemon juice, salt, or garlic as desired.

Store the aioli in an airtight container, refrigerated, for up to 2 days.

TIP: If for some reason your aioli breaks or doesn't emulsify properly, no need to toss out the whole batch. Start with a clean bowl and a new egg yolk. Add a pinch of salt and start whisking in new oil, a drop at a time. Once the new yolk and oil have a smooth emulsification going, start whisking in your broken aioli, one drop at a time, until it's all incorporated.

AIOLI VARIATIONS

- **HERBY:** Add ½ cup [20 g] of any of the following fresh herbs, finely chopped: parsley, mint, tarragon, chervil, or basil. Alternatively, add 2 to 3 Tbsp prepared pesto (page 19) or swap part of the plain oil for Basil Oil (or other herb oil; page 31).

- **SMOKY:** Add 1 tsp of pimentón or smoked paprika.

- **BRINY:** Add 1 to 2 Tbsp drained chopped capers, cornichons, olives, or anchovies or a combination of these ingredients.

- **SPICY:** Add a few drops of Sriracha sauce, a hot sauce like Tabasco, or the adobo sauce from a can of chipotle chiles in adobo. Alternatively, for a different kind of kick, add a few teaspoons of prepared horseradish or wasabi.

- **HARISSA:** Add 1 to 2 Tbsp prepared harissa.

- **MUSTARD:** Add 2 to 3 Tbsp of any kind of mustard.

- **RUSSIAN DRESSING:** Add 2 to 3 Tbsp Fire-Roasted Ketchup (page 23) or store-bought ketchup, and one or two very finely chopped cornichons.

FIRE-ROASTED KETCHUP

No one here will tell you that Heinz Ketchup is anything less than perfect. That said, sometimes it's nice to try to make your own condiments, especially when you're going for something with a little more smoke and tang than the original.

1½ lbs [680 g] plum tomatoes

¼ medium red onion

1 garlic clove, unpeeled

¼ cup [60 ml] apple cider vinegar

2 Tbsp granulated sugar

1 tsp whole mustard seeds

4 whole cloves

¼ tsp ground cinnamon

¼ tsp ground cumin

¼ tsp celery salt

3 whole black peppercorns

¼ tsp dry mustard powder

¼ tsp kosher salt

Heat your grill to medium-high and cook the tomatoes, onion, and garlic until all the vegetables are evenly charred, 8 to 10 minutes total. When the garlic is cool enough to handle, remove the skin. Transfer the grilled vegetables to a blender and blend until very smooth. Strain the mixture through a fine mesh sieve, pressing on the solids to release as much juice as possible, into a medium saucepan. Discard the solids. Bring the juice to a boil and then lower the heat and simmer until the tomato mixture has thickened, about 30 minutes.

Meanwhile, combine the vinegar, sugar, spices, and salt in a small saucepan. Bring to a simmer, stirring to dissolve the sugar. Turn off the heat. When the tomato juice has thickened, strain the spiced vinegar into the tomato mixture and simmer for another 20 to 30 minutes, until the ketchup is thick but still pourable. Cool completely before serving or storing. The ketchup will keep, refrigerated, for 2 to 3 months.

INDOOR METHOD: Preheat the oven to 400°F [200°C]. On a foil- or parchment-lined baking sheet, lay out the tomatoes, onion, and garlic. Roast for 15 to 20 minutes, until the tomatoes slump and start to give off juice and the onion and garlic are soft. Proceed as directed above.

SLATHERS, DIPS, DRIZZLES, AND BASICS

CHARRED BEET HUMMUS

This change-of-pace hummus doubles down on the earthiness of the beets, by adding a layer of subtle smokiness. The finished dip is a gorgeous color and pretty addictive.

3 small to medium beets
One 15.5-oz [445-g] can chickpeas
½ cup [60 ml] plus 2 Tbsp extra-virgin olive oil
1 tsp kosher salt, plus more as needed
1 lemon, halved
3 garlic cloves, or more to taste, unpeeled
¼ cup [55 g] tahini
Feta cheese, for garnish (optional)
Pita wedges or Kale Chips (page 85),
   for serving

To prepare the beets, scrub them well, trim off the tops and any long root ends, and wrap them in two layers of aluminum foil.

Drain and rinse the chickpeas under cold water. In a small bowl, toss them with 2 Tbsp olive oil and sprinkle with salt.

Heat grill to medium-high and put a mesh grill topper or a piece of aluminum foil to one side. If using a charcoal grill, place the packet with the beets next to the coals. If using a gas grill, place the beets on the grate. Transfer the chickpeas to the grill topper. Grill the beets, chickpeas, lemon halves, cut-side down, and the garlic cloves, shaking the chickpeas every few minutes until they're brown in spots, 10 to 15 minutes. Remove the lemons when the cut sides are caramelized and the fruit starts to easily give up its juice, about 8 minutes. Similarly, remove the garlic when the peels are a bit charred and the cloves are soft when squeezed, 8 to 10 minutes. Cook the beets, flipping once halfway through, until a knife easily pierces them through the foil, about 30 minutes total.

Transfer the charred chickpeas to the bowl of a food processor or blender. When the garlic is cool enough to handle, remove the skins and add the garlic to the food processor. When the beets are cool enough to handle, peel them (the skins should slip right off), coarsely chop them, and add them to the food processor as well. Add the juice from the grilled lemons along with the ½ cup olive oil, tahini, and 1 tsp salt. Blend until smooth. Serve warm or at room temperature, garnished with crumbled feta cheese (if using), alongside grilled pita wedges.

The hummus can be made up to 3 days in advance. Keep refrigerated and bring to room temperature before using.

TAHINI SAUCE

Tahini sauce is incredibly versatile. Like adding cheese or mayonnaise to a dish, it adds a decadent creaminess with a little more complexity and without all the dairy. That said, it's also a little fiddly. Amounts given are approximate— you may use anywhere between 3 and 6 Tbsp of water to get the right consistency, and depending on the juiciness of your lemon, half might be enough, or you might need a whole one to counter the bitterness of the tahini. Play around and taste as you go. The finished product should be creamy and pourable, and taste balanced between the nutty sesame paste, the acid from the lemon, and the salt, with that background hit of garlic to round it out.

¼ cup [60 ml] tahini
Zest and juice of half or a whole lemon
1 small garlic clove, finely grated
Kosher salt

In a small bowl, stir together the tahini, lemon zest and juice, garlic, and ½ tsp of salt. Add water 1 Tbsp at a time until the mixture is smooth and creamy. Taste, and add more lemon, salt, or water if necessary. Serve immediately or let sit at room temperature for several hours. The sauce will also keep, refrigerated, for up to a week. Bring to room temperature and add more water if necessary before serving.

SMOKY EGGPLANT DIP

This dip is close to Yotam Ottolenghi's, although here we let that eggplant get hot and velvety on the grill. It makes the most of the biggest, sturdiest kinds of deep purple eggplants and marries that silky flesh with nutty tahini and sweet-tangy pomegranate molasses. It's a key component of the Eggplant Sandwiches with Pickles and Hard-Boiled Eggs (page 62), is great with grilled pita wedges, and makes an excellent dip for fresh, grilled, or pickled carrots, radishes, and fennel.

One 1½- to 2-lb [680- to 900-g] eggplant
⅓ cup [80 ml] tahini
¼ cup [60 ml] water
1 garlic clove, grated, plus more as needed
3 Tbsp finely chopped flat-leaf parsley
1 Tbsp fresh lemon juice, plus more as needed
2 tsp pomegranate molasses, plus more as needed
Kosher salt
2 Tbsp pomegranate seeds, for garnish (optional)

Heat your grill to medium-high heat. Put the whole eggplant directly on the grill grate, turning often until it has blackened on all sides and has begun to collapse, about 15 minutes total. Transfer to a bowl. When the eggplant has cooled slightly, scoop the flesh into a colander, letting it drain for 25 to 30 minutes. Discard the blackened skin.

In a medium bowl, mix the eggplant flesh with the tahini, water, garlic, parsley, lemon juice, pomegranate molasses, and a big pinch of salt. Taste and add more lemon juice, garlic, pomegranate molasses, or salt as needed. Serve warm or at room temperature, with pomegranate seeds scattered on top for garnish, if using. This dip can be made up to 2 days in advance; bring to room temperature before using.

INDOOR METHOD: If using a gas stove, line the stovetop with foil to make for easier cleanup. Turn one burner to high heat. With sturdy tongs, hold the eggplant over the burner, turning and rotating often, until the entire eggplant is charred black and soft, about 15 minutes. Alternatively, preheat your broiler and prick the eggplant several times with a sharp knife. On a foil-lined baking sheet, broil the eggplant, turning it every few minutes, until it's completely charred and collapsing. Proceed as directed above.

TERIYAKI SAUCE

Never thought about making your own teriyaki sauce? This five-ingredient version from the Canal House should change that. We use it here for mush-rooms and tofu, but it's also a dynamite marinade for salmon.

1 cup [240 ml] soy sauce
1 cup [240 ml] mirin
1 cup [180 g] brown sugar
One 2-in [5-cm] piece fresh ginger, peeled
    and sliced
3 garlic cloves, peeled

Combine the soy sauce, mirin, brown sugar, ginger, and garlic in a small saucepan. Bring to a boil, reduce the heat to low, and simmer until the sauce is slightly thickened, 30 to 40 minutes. Move from the heat and remove and discard the ginger and garlic. The teriyaki sauce will keep, refrigerated, in an airtight jar or container for 2 to 3 months.

PICKLES TWO WAYS

Quick pickles are easy to make and their fresh, salty bite is a perfect contrast to slightly sweet, soft grilled vegetables. Often they add just the right unexpected flavor or texture to take a dish from ordinary to impressive.

PICKLED ONIONS OR SHALLOTS

This quick pickling method, which requires no heat, also works well for cucumbers, radishes, and jalapeño chiles.

¼ cup [60 ml] white vinegar
¼ cup [60 ml] water
2 tsp kosher salt
½ tsp sugar
½ red onion or 2 small shallots, peeled and sliced into very thin slices or rings

In a jar big enough to hold all of the ingredients, combine the vinegar, water, salt, and sugar and shake well to dissolve the sugar and salt. Add the onion and let sit for at least 30 minutes before serving. Pickled onions will keep, refrigerated, for up to 7 days.

PICKLED CARROTS

This other method for quick refrigerator pickles works well for a variety of produce, from other roots like turnips and beets to summery veggies like green beans and asparagus.

2 carrots
⅓ cup [80 ml] white vinegar
⅓ cup [80 ml] water
1 Tbsp granulated sugar
½ Tbsp kosher salt

Peel the carrots and cut into the desired shape (thin matchsticks for the Mushroom and Tofu Spring Rolls, page 114, and thin planks for the Zucchini Tartines with Goat Cheese and Pickled Carrots, page 67). In a small saucepan, bring the vinegar, water, sugar, and salt to a boil. Add the carrots and boil for 3 minutes more. Transfer the carrots and brine to a container or jar. The carrot pickles will keep, refrigerated in the brine, for up to 7 days.

BASIL OIL

Basil oil is incredibly easy to make, and it pays off in such big ways. It can be used to marinate zucchini, dress Halloumi and tomatoes, toss with pasta, slather on sandwiches, or even whisk into aioli for an herbaceous riff. If you want to be fancy about it, line a fine mesh strainer with slightly damp cheesecloth or a paper coffee filter and strain the oil after you have puréed it for a clear, bright finished product.

2 cups [24 g] basil leaves, packed
1 cup [240 ml] extra-virgin olive oil

In a medium bowl make an ice bath. Bring a small pot of water to a boil. Add the basil to the boiling water and blanch just until the leaves turn bright green, about 30 seconds. Drain and plunge the basil into the ice bath (or run under cold water immediately). Once cool, gather the leaves into a ball and wring out as much water as possible. Transfer to a blender and add the olive oil. Blend until smooth. Set aside at room temperature if using the same day; otherwise refrigerate. Basil oil can be made up to 3 days ahead. Bring to room temperature before using.

VARIATIONS: Feel free to experiment, as any herb can be used to create flavored oil. Soft herbs like parsley, cilantro, and mint should be blanched, following the method used above for basil oil. For heartier herbs like rosemary or oregano, in a small saucepan over low heat, gently heat the oil with a few whole sprigs of the herb for 5 or 6 minutes. Remove from the heat and let cool.

SLATHERS, DIPS, DRIZZLES, AND BASICS

ROASTED GARLIC

Roasted garlic is incredibly versatile. You can spread it directly on grilled bread with a pinch of salt for an easy starter or side or stir it into hummus, white bean dip, or salad dressings to give them a mellow garlic flavor.

1 head of garlic
1 Tbsp extra-virgin olive oil
Kosher salt

Preheat the oven to 350°F [180°C]. Cut the top ½ in [12 mm] off of the head of garlic so that the tops of the cloves are exposed. Drizzle with olive oil, sprinkle lightly with salt, and wrap the garlic in foil. Roast the garlic in the oven for 45 to 55 minutes, until the cloves are soft when pressed. When cool enough to handle, pinch the cloves from their skins and discard skins. Store, in an airtight container, refrigerated, for up to 2 days.

FRIED SHALLOTS

All I can say about fried shallots is that you should make more than you need. They grace everything they touch with just the right amount of golden, salty, oniony (but not too oniony) crispness. If you're going for gluten-free, substitute rice flour, or skip the coating entirely.

3 medium shallots, cut into ⅛-in [3-mm] slices
3 Tbsp Wondra or all-purpose flour
Kosher salt
½ cup [120 ml] vegetable oil

In a small bowl, toss the shallot rings with the flour and a pinch of salt. Line a plate with paper towels. In a medium skillet, heat the oil over high heat. When the oil is shimmering, add the shallots, stirring often until they are evenly golden brown. (Watch carefully toward the end!) Transfer to the plate and sprinkle immediately with another pinch of salt. These can be prepared several hours ahead of time but should be used the same day they are fried. Leave uncovered at room temperature.

CHARRED CHICKPEAS

Charred chickpeas are a great way to add heft and protein to many of the vegetable dishes in this book. Unlike other beans, they hold their structure well while becoming crisp and roasted. Serve charred chickpeas as a snack with drinks or add them to any of the dishes here to add more substance and crunch.

2 cups [320 g] cooked chickpeas or one 15.5-oz [445-g] can chickpeas, drained and rinsed

2 to 3 Tbsp extra-virgin olive oil

Kosher salt

Smoked paprika (optional)

In a small bowl, toss the chickpeas with 2 Tbsp olive oil and sprinkle with salt and smoked paprika, if using. Transfer them to a grill topper. (Tip: you may have to wrap the topper's edges in foil so the chickpeas won't roll off.)

Heat your grill to medium and place the grill topper on the grate. Cook, shaking the chickpeas every few minutes until they're deeply brown—or even black in spots—and crisp, 10 to 15 minutes.

Charred chickpeas are best the day they're made but can be stored for a day in an air-tight container or resealable bag at room temperature.

TIP: No grill topper? Use foil instead, with the edges curved up slightly to make a shallow bowl. The chickpeas will still roast; they'll just have a slightly less smoky flavor.

GRILLED BREAD

Grilled bread is a natural pairing for many of the dishes in this book, and croutons and crisp bread crumbs add a welcome crunch. Any bread benefits from a quick toast over a fire, from substantial crusty slices (my favorite) to hamburger rolls for veggie burgers (pages 102 and 104) to pillowy pitas.

4 to 8 slices or pieces of crusty bread, pita, naan, or hamburger buns

2 to 3 Tbsp extra-virgin olive oil

Kosher salt

Brush one or both sides of the bread with olive oil, sprinkle with salt, and grill for 1 to 2 minutes over medium-low heat, until the bread is crisp and has lovely grill marks. Grilled bread can be made in advance but should be used the day it's made. Alternatively, it can be added to the cool part of the grill during the final minutes of cooking the rest of your meal.

INDOOR METHOD: Preheat the oven to 375°F [190°C]. Lay the bread slices on a baking sheet in a single layer. Brush with oil, sprinkle with salt, and toast, turning once, until both sides are golden, about 15 minutes.

GRILLED CROUTONS

Often croutons have the ability to turn a collection of vegetables into a substantial, satisfying panzanella salad. Croutons are best the day that they're made but can be made up to a day in advance. Store in an airtight container or resealable plastic bag at room temperature. Also, stale bread works well here, as it soaks up oil even better than fresh bread, which in turn means crunchier croutons.

3 or 4 slices crusty bread
4 to 5 Tbsp extra-virgin olive oil
Kosher salt

Cut the bread into ½- to 1-in [12-mm to 2.5-cm] cubes. In a bowl, toss with olive oil, gently squeezing the bread so that the cubes absorb as much oil as possible. Season lightly with salt and then, using a grill topper, grill the cubes over medium-low heat until they are well toasted.

INDOOR METHOD: Preheat the oven to 375°F [190°C]. Prepare the croutons as directed through seasoning. Then, on a foil- or parchment-lined baking sheet, toast the croutons until crisp and golden, tossing once or twice, about 15 minutes.

TWO METHODS FOR GRILLED BREAD CRUMBS

Like croutons, bread crumbs add that essential crunch to any dish and are a perfect complement to soft, sweet grilled vegetables.

3 or 4 slices crusty bread
4 to 5 Tbsp extra-virgin olive oil or unsalted butter
Kosher salt
Shallots, garlic, or other aromatics (optional)

There are two methods to make bread crumbs. The FIRST METHOD is to make croutons as described on page 37, toasting them until they are quite brown and crisp. Then with a large knife coarsely chop them (which is messy) or put them in a resealable plastic bag and crush them with a rolling pin until they're the desired size (which is less messy). The SECOND METHOD is used for the bread crumbs in Smoked Beets with Dill Yogurt Dressing and Rye Bread Crumbs (page 123) and with the Cauliflower Roast with Anchovy Bread Crumbs (page 56) and goes as follows: tear by hand or pulse bread in a food processor until you have a cup or two of small crumbs. Heat oil or butter, or both (along with shallots, garlic, etc.), in a skillet and toast the bread crumbs, stirring often, until they are golden and crunchy. Drain on paper towels.

TOASTED NUTS AND SEEDS

To be honest, when I toast nuts, I use the path of least resistance. If I have to use a skillet for another part of the recipe later, I'll toast them in that skillet. If not, I don't.

1 cup nuts or seeds such as peanuts, almonds, sunflower seeds, pumpkin seeds, etc.

To toast nuts or seeds in a skillet, heat a clean, dry skillet over medium heat. Add the seeds or nuts and stir often until they smell toasty and have turned a bit golden, 2 to 8 minutes, depending on size. When they are done, transfer them to a bowl or plate so the heat from the pan does not take them from golden to burned. Alternatively, spread the nuts or seeds out on a foil-lined baking sheet and toast them in the oven at 350°F [180°C], or even more often, in the toaster oven until they're golden. The key is to watch carefully, as they can turn on you in a flash.

TOMATOES, BRASSICAS, SQUASH, AND LEAVES

BURST AND FRESH TOMATOES WITH HALLOUMI AND BASIL OIL

This dish is almost like a deconstructed, summery pizza (in the best possible way). It's also endlessly adaptable. You can swap the tomatoes for grilled peaches or watermelon or switch out the basil oil for mint or fresh oregano oil. Serve it over a tangle of arugula or pile it onto freshly grilled Flatbread (page 136). It all works.

1 pint [about 300 g] cherry tomatoes

2 Tbsp extra-virgin olive oil,
   plus more for brushing

Kosher salt

Freshly ground black pepper

Two 8.8-oz [250-g] packages Halloumi cheese

Basil Oil (page 31)

Toss the tomatoes with 2 Tbsp olive oil, salt, and pepper. Heat the grill to medium, and using a grill topper, cook until the tomatoes start to burst, about 5 minutes. Transfer to a plate. Cut the Halloumi into planks. Brush each plank well with olive oil, season with salt and freshly ground pepper, and grill the cheese until you can see grill marks and it starts to melt, 1 to 2 minutes. Flip the planks and cook for another 1 to 2 minutes. Arrange the cheese on plates, add the tomatoes, and drizzle liberally with basil oil. Serve immediately.

INDOOR METHOD: Preheat the oven to 300°F [150°C]. On a rimmed baking sheet, coat the tomatoes with 1 Tbsp of olive oil and sprinkle with salt and pepper. Roast the tomatoes in a single layer until they start to slump and the flavor concentrates, about 45 minutes. Heat a cast-iron skillet over medium heat. Instead of brushing the Halloumi with oil, pat it very dry with paper towels. Add 2 Tbsp oil to the skillet. When the oil is shimmering, fry the cheese until both sides are golden brown. Proceed with the remainder of the recipe as directed.

GRILLED SHAKSHUKA

This version of shakshuka, eggs cooked directly in a spicy tomato sauce, gets a double hit of smoky flavor, first from grilling the vegetables, and then from earthy canned chipotle chiles in adobo sauce. Don't skimp on any of the components—the creamy cool feta, the fresh cilantro, and the spicy sauce make this a killer brunch dish. Be sure to serve it with plenty of grilled bread on the side.

7 plum tomatoes

1 small yellow onion, peeled and halved

1 Anaheim chile or red bell pepper

2 garlic cloves, unpeeled

1 tsp ground cumin

1 tsp pimentón or smoked paprika

1 tsp dried oregano

1 canned chipotle chile in adobo, plus 1 tsp or more adobo sauce

1 tsp kosher salt, plus more for sprinkling

Freshly ground black pepper

Eight slices crusty bread, each 1 in [2.5 cm] thick

2 Tbsp extra-virgin olive oil

4 eggs

1 cup [about 8 oz/250 g] crumbled feta cheese

2 Tbsp finely chopped fresh cilantro, for garnish

Heat the grill to medium-high. Place the tomatoes, onion, Anaheim chile, and garlic on the grill. Cook the vegetables, turning every 2 to 3 minutes, until they are evenly charred on all sides and beginning to soften. When the tomatoes start to blister and drip juice, after 8 or 9 minutes, transfer them to a bowl and let cool slightly. When the chile is charred on all sides, transfer it to a separate small bowl and cover the bowl tightly with plastic wrap. Set aside. When the onion is evenly charred and softened, about 12 minutes, transfer it to the bowl with the tomatoes. Remove the garlic when the skins are charred and the cloves are soft when pressed, about 8 or 9 minutes, and squeeze the garlic cloves from their peels into the tomatoes and onions. Keep the grill hot, either by turning a gas grill to high or by adding more coals to a charcoal grill.

When the tomatoes are cool enough to handle, slip off the skins (they should peel off easily; don't worry about getting every last bit) and put the tomatoes in a blender. Add the onion, coarsely chopped, and the garlic. When the chile has cooled, remove and discard the skin, stem, and seeds. Then add the chile to the blender, along with the cumin, pimentón, oregano, the chipotle chile and sauce, and 1 tsp salt. Blend until almost smooth. Taste and adjust the sauce for salt and pepper. For a spicier sauce, add more chipotles.

Prepare the bread. Lay the slices on a baking sheet and brush both sides with oil and sprinkle lightly with salt.

CONTINUED

Pour the sauce into a 10-in [25-cm] cast-iron skillet and place back on the grill over high heat. Let simmer until the sauce is slightly thickened, about 10 minutes. With the sauce bubbling, make four divots in the surface with the back of a spoon. Carefully crack an egg into each dip (if you're nervous about this, crack each egg into a small bowl and gently slide the egg into the sauce divot). Cover the grill and cook until the white has set but the yolk is still runny, 8 to 10 minutes. Check often toward the end so you don't cook your yolks. While you're waiting for the eggs to set, prepare the bread on a cooler part of the grill until it's toasted and has grill marks on both sides.

When the eggs are set, divide both eggs and sauce among four shallow bowls, taking care not to disturb the yolks. Top with feta and garnish with cilantro. Serve immediately with grilled bread alongside.

INDOOR METHOD: Substitute one 28-oz [825-ml] can whole, peeled tomatoes for the fresh ones. Chop the onion, Anaheim chile, and garlic. In a cast-iron skillet over medium-high heat, sauté the onion, chile, and garlic until the onion is translucent and the chile is soft, about 10 minutes. Add the tomatoes, crushing them slightly. Add the cumin, pimentón, oregano, chipotle, and adobo sauce. Bring to a simmer, taste, and adjust the seasoning. If you prefer a chunkier sauce, simmer for 10 minutes or so and then add the eggs. For a smoother sauce, carefully transfer the sauce to a blender, blend, and return it to the pan. Let the sauce simmer 10 minutes and then add the eggs, covering the pan with a lid. Proceed with the remainder of the recipe as directed.

GRILLED GAZPACHO

As someone who thinks most gazpacho-eating experiences come too close to eating salsa by the spoonful, I find this gazpacho creamy and satisfying. Double or triple the recipe to feed a crowd.

4 plum tomatoes
¼ red onion
1 red bell pepper
1 garlic clove, unpeeled
¼ cup [60 ml] extra-virgin olive oil
1 Tbsp sherry vinegar, plus more as needed
1 tsp kosher salt, plus more as needed
Freshly ground black pepper
3 small Persian or ½ English cucumber, finely diced
¼ cup [10 g] finely chopped flat-leaf parsley
1 green onion, thinly sliced, for garnish
1 avocado, diced, for garnish (optional)

Heat the grill to medium-high. Add the tomatoes, onion, bell pepper, and garlic to the grill. If the garlic is in danger of falling through the grate, use a grill topper or put it on a small piece of foil. As each vegetable begins to char and take on color, turn it so it has even grill marks all around. When the tomato skins have blistered and the juices start to drip, about 9 minutes, remove from the grill and transfer to a bowl. Similarly, turn the onion and pepper until they are evenly marked and cooked through. When the onion is done, add it to the bowl with the tomatoes. When the pepper is charred and soft, transfer it to a separate small bowl, and cover the bowl tightly with plastic wrap. Remove the garlic when the skin is blackened and the clove is soft when pressed

When the tomatoes are cool enough to handle, slip off the skins (they should be easy to remove), and add the tomatoes, whole, to a blender. Coarsely chop the onion, discarding the stem, and add to the blender with the tomatoes. When the pepper is cool enough to handle, remove and discard the skin, stem, and seeds. Coarsely tear into a few pieces and add to the blender as well. Add the garlic (discard the skin), olive oil, vinegar, 1 tsp of salt, and several grinds of pepper and blend until smooth.

Transfer to a bowl, add in ⅔ of the cucumber, and stir. Taste and add more vinegar, salt, or pepper if desired. Divide the soup among serving bowls. Garnish with the reserved cucumber, parsley, green onion, and avocado, if using, and serve.

INDOOR METHOD: While you could cook all of the vegetables under the broiler, this particular recipe doesn't translate very well to indoor cooking methods. Seek out a different gazpacho recipe.

ROMANESCO WITH ROMESCO SAUCE

While the pepper- and nut-based romesco sauce was originally made in northern Spain to accompany fish, it's incredibly versatile. The play on words makes it hard to resist serving it with the funny green cauliflower, romanesco, but it is also delicious with thick eggplant steaks or grilled potatoes. I usually serve it as a dipping sauce on the side, but you can also spoon it over the romanesco and—to kick the flavors up a notch—top the whole thing with strips of crispy prosciutto or Serrano ham.

2 heads of romanesco or 1 head of cauliflower, trimmed and cut into large florets

2 Tbsp extra-virgin olive oil

Kosher salt

Manchego or Parmesan cheese, for garnish

Romesco Sauce (recipe follows)

Preheat the grill to medium-high. In a large bowl, toss the romanesco florets with the olive oil and season with salt. Cook the romanesco until it's well charred and tender, about 4 minutes per side.

Transfer the romanesco to a platter, garnish with the cheese, and serve with the romesco sauce alongside. Serve warm or at room temperature.

INDOOR METHOD: Prepare the romesco sauce as directed. Preheat the broiler. Trim, oil, and season the romanesco as directed. On a foil-lined baking sheet, broil the romanesco, tossing a few times, until the florets are well charred in spots and tender, 8 to 10 minutes. Proceed with the remainder of the recipe as directed.

CONTINUED

ROMESCO SAUCE

Romesco, a substantial, nutty, peppery sauce, has the ability to turn any grilled vegetable, plus bread, into a meal.

2 red bell peppers
1 garlic clove, peeled
½ cup [70 g] roasted unsalted almonds
⅓ cup [80 ml] tomato purée
2 Tbsp chopped fresh flat-leaf parsley
1 Tbsp sherry vinegar
1 tsp pimentón
1 tsp kosher salt
⅓ cup [80 ml] extra-virgin olive oil

Heat your grill to medium-high and add the peppers. Turn occasionally until charred on all sides and soft, about 10 minutes total. Transfer to a bowl and cover tightly with plastic wrap. Set aside.

In a food processor or blender, combine the garlic, almonds, tomato purée, parsley, vinegar, pimentón, and salt. Set aside.

When the peppers are cool enough to handle, remove and discard the skins, stems, and seeds. Halve the peppers. Add the peppers to the food processor and pulse until the ingredients are well combined. Add the oil and blend again until smooth. Romesco will keep, refrigerated, in an airtight jar or container for 1 week.

INDOOR METHOD: Preheat the broiler. On a foil-lined baking sheet, broil the peppers, turning every 3 to 4 minutes, until all sides are charred and the peppers are soft and collapsing. Transfer the peppers to a bowl, cover with plastic wrap, and proceed as above.

BROCCOLI STEAKS WITH CHEDDAR BEER DIPPING SAUCE AND GRILLED ONION RINGS

While the juices won't run out like a steak, this charred broccoli, Cheddar cheese, and onion ring combo goes pretty perfectly with a cold beer. Use a flavorful beer, such as an India pale ale (IPA), for the sauce and sip the rest while the veggies are cooking.

FOR THE CHEDDAR BEER DIPPING SAUCE

2 Tbsp unsalted butter
2 Tbsp all-purpose flour
¾ cup [180 ml] whole milk
1 cup [80 g] coarsely grated sharp Cheddar cheese
¼ cup [60 ml] beer
2 Tbsp Dijon mustard
2 tsp Worcestershire sauce
1 tsp kosher salt

FOR THE BROCCOLI STEAKS

2 large heads of broccoli
⅓ cup [80 ml] extra-virgin olive oil
Kosher salt

FOR THE GRILLED ONION RINGS

½ cup [35 g] all-purpose flour
1 tsp kosher salt
¼ tsp cayenne pepper
3 eggs, lightly beaten
3 cups [150 g] panko bread crumbs
1 red onion, cut into ¾-in [2-cm] slices
Extra-virgin olive oil, for drizzling
Flaky salt, such as Maldon, for finishing

TO MAKE THE CHEDDAR BEER DIPPING SAUCE: In a medium saucepan, melt the butter over medium heat. Add the flour, stirring constantly with a whisk until the mixture starts to turn golden, about 5 minutes. Slowly drizzle in the milk, constantly whisking to avoid lumps, until it's all incorporated. Add the cheese in batches, waiting for each to melt before adding the next. When all of the cheese is incorporated and the sauce is smooth, add the beer, mustard, Worcestershire sauce, and salt. Bring the sauce to a simmer and then turn off the heat while you prepare and grill your vegetables.

TO MAKE THE BROCCOLI STEAKS: Cut the heads in halves or quarters lengthwise through the stem to create 2 or 4 "steaks," depending on the size. Brush all over with olive oil and sprinkle liberally with salt.

CONTINUED

TO MAKE THE GRILLED ONION RINGS: Set up your dredging station. In a shallow medium bowl or dish, such as a pie plate, stir together the flour, salt, and cayenne pepper. Put the eggs in another bowl. Pour the panko into a third bowl. Separate the onion slices into rings and dip each ring first into the egg, shaking off excess, then into the flour, then back into the egg, and then finally into the panko, pressing to adhere the crumbs so each ring has an even coating. Lay the onion slices on a lightly oiled baking sheet and drizzle with olive oil.

TO ASSEMBLE: Heat your grill to high on one side and medium-low on the other. If using a charcoal grill, pile the coals to one side. Cook the broccoli over the hot part until it's well charred and the florets are crispy, about 6 minutes. Flip and cook for another 3 or 4 minutes. At the same time, and using a light hand so as not to disturb the coating, grill the onion rings over the cooler part of the grill until the crust is fully golden and the onions are soft, about 5 minutes per side.

If necessary, reheat the cheese dipping sauce over low heat, stirring, until warm and smooth.

To serve, heap the broccoli onto a platter or divide among four plates. Spoon the cheese sauce over the steaks and pile the onion rings on top. Sprinkle with flaky salt to finish. Serve immediately.

INDOOR METHOD: Prepare the cheese dipping sauce as directed. Preheat the oven to 450°F [230°C]. On a baking sheet, cut, oil, and season the broccoli as directed. Prepare the onion rings as directed and divide between two baking sheets to avoid crowding. Cook the broccoli and onion rings, flipping everything once halfway through. The onion rings will be done when they're evenly brown and crisp. The broccoli is done when the tops are deep brown, very crisp, and the stems are tender. If the broccoli is getting cooked through but is not sufficiently brown or crisp, remove the onion rings from the oven, put the baking sheet with the broccoli on the top rack, directly under the broiler, and broil for 3 to 4 minutes. Prepare the remainder of the recipe as directed.

SERVES 4

CHARRED BROCCOLI AND WHITE BEAN CROSTINI

These crostini are delicious and filling, a great lunch or a perfect start to a light meal. The bean purée is very forgiving—the beans can be dried or canned, cooked a day or two before, blended with more garlic or less. It also works well as a dip for raw or grilled crudités, just make sure it's well seasoned. Additionally, crostini are incredibly flexible. Any of the flatbread topping suggestions (page 138) would work just as well piled on lightly toasted baguette slices.

1 head of broccoli or 2 bunches of broccoli rabe or broccolini
3 Tbsp [45 ml] extra-virgin olive oil
Kosher salt
Freshly ground black pepper
Crostini (see page 135)
White Bean Purée (recipe follows)
1 tsp lemon zest, for garnish

Trim the end from the head of broccoli or broccolini, as well as any knobby bits. Cut into long, thin florets, about ½ in [12 mm] each. Toss with the olive oil, salt, and freshly ground pepper.

Build a medium-hot fire in a charcoal grill or heat a gas grill to high. Place a wire cooling rack or grill topper over the grill grate. Place the broccoli on top of the rack and grill until the tops of the florets are charred and stems are slightly browned and cooked through but not overly soft, 6 or 7 minutes, tossing and flipping occasionally.

Prepare the crostini up to the point where they are taken off the grill. Spread each of the crostini with a tablespoon or so of the bean purée and top with grilled broccoli florets (trim if they seem unwieldy and will be difficult to eat). Garnish with lemon zest. Serve immediately.

INDOOR METHOD: Prepare the crostini as directed on page 135. Preheat the broiler. Trim, oil, and season the broccoli as directed. Scatter on a foil-lined baking sheet and broil until the tops are charred and stems are tender and brown in spots, about 7 minutes. Proceed with the remainder of the recipe as directed.

WHITE BEAN PURÉE

1 head of garlic

One 15.5-oz [445-g] can white beans, such
as great Northern or cannellini, or 2 cups
cooked white beans such as cannellini, lima,
or corona beans, drained, liquid reserved

2 Tbsp extra-virgin olive oil

Kosher salt

Preheat the oven to 350°F [180°C]. Wrap the
garlic in aluminum foil and roast for 35 to
40 minutes, until soft when pressed. When
cool enough to handle, slip the garlic from the
skins and set aside.

Next, combine the beans, 2 or 3 cloves of the
roasted garlic, the olive oil, 2 Tbsp of water (if
using canned beans) or the reserved liquid, and
a pinch of salt in a blender or food processor.
Blend until very smooth, adding more water or
bean liquid as necessary. The final purée should
be creamy and spreadable, like smooth mashed
potatoes. Taste and adjust the seasoning. Serve
this spread on crostini, as in the preceding recipe; in a bowl alongside crudités; or even spread
on toast with smoked salmon or trout. The bean
purée can be made up to 3 days in advance;
refrigerate and bring to room temperature
before serving.

CAULIFLOWER ROAST WITH ANCHOVY BREAD CRUMBS

While this cauliflower roast looks impressive, it couldn't be easier to get on the table. Roasting the vegetable whole makes it more forgiving than grilling the florets individually.

One 1½-lb [680-g] head of cauliflower
½ cup [120 ml] extra-virgin olive oil
Kosher salt
8 anchovy fillets
3 garlic cloves, peeled and finely chopped
1 shallot, peeled and finely chopped
1 tsp lemon zest
¼ tsp crushed red pepper flakes
1 cup [40 g] fresh bread crumbs (see page 38)
½ cup [20 g] finely chopped flat-leaf parsley
Lemon wedges, for serving
Flaky salt, such as Maldon, for serving

Heat your grill to medium, so it's around 400°F [200°C] with the top closed. Trim the leaves and the very bottom part of the stem off the cauliflower and discard. Set the head on a sheet of heavy-duty aluminum foil. Brush the cauliflower all over with ¼ cup [60 ml] oil and sprinkle liberally with kosher salt. Transfer the cauliflower, on the foil, to the grill, cover, and let cook, undisturbed. After 20 minutes, begin checking for doneness. The cauliflower will be done when the whole head is golden and a knife can slip into the vegetable with little resistance, but before it gets mushy or the cauliflower starts to break apart when squeezed. It

could take up to 35 minutes to finish cooking, depending on the size of the head and the temperature of the grill. If it requires more time, just cover the grill and wait a few more minutes before checking again.

Meanwhile, make the bread crumbs. In a large sauté pan or skillet, heat the remaining ¼ cup [60 ml] olive oil over medium heat. When the oil starts to shimmer, add the anchovies, garlic, shallot, lemon zest, red pepper flakes, and bread crumbs. Cook, stirring often, until the anchovies have dissolved and the garlic, shallot, and bread crumbs are golden. Turn off the heat and stir in the parsley. Set aside.

When the cauliflower is done, transfer it to a large plate or platter. Use two forks to pry the head apart into several large pieces. Squeeze a wedge of lemon over the cauliflower and sprinkle with coarse, flaky salt. Pile the bread crumbs in the center. Serve immediately.

INDOOR METHOD: Preheat the oven to 400°F [200°C]. Trim, oil, and season the cauliflower as directed. Place in a cast-iron skillet and cover tightly with foil. Roast the cauliflower for 30 minutes. Remove the foil, and roast for an additional 30 to 45 minutes, until the entire cauliflower is tender and deeply brown. Proceed with the recipe as directed.

CAULIFLOWER STEAKS WITH TAHINI

This dish is so satisfying. The nutty richness of the tahini sauce and the sweetness of the pomegranate molasses balance out and make this vegan main dish feel substantial. It's so good and simple that I'd nominate it to be the poster child of vegetable grilling right now.

One 1½-lb [680-g] head of cauliflower

1 tsp kosher salt, plus more as needed

¼ tsp chili powder

1 tsp pimentón or smoked paprika

2 Tbsp extra-virgin olive oil

¼ cup [55 g] tahini

Zest and juice of ½ lemon, plus more juice as needed

½ tsp freshly ground black pepper

2 Tbsp chopped fresh mint

2 Tbsp chopped fresh parsley

2 Tbsp chopped fresh cilantro

½ green onion, green part only, thinly sliced

3 Tbsp pomegranate molasses

Starting at the top center of the cauliflower, cut two slices lengthwise through the stem end, each 1 in [2.5 cm] thick. If desired, use all of the remaining cauliflower as well, cutting it into large florets for this dish. (They are equally delicious; they just don't have the steak-like presentation.) Otherwise reserve for another use.

In a small bowl, mix together ½ tsp salt, the chili powder, and the pimentón. Brush the cauliflower with the olive oil so it's coated on all sides and then liberally season with the spice mixture. Heat your grill to medium-high. Grill the cauliflower on the hottest part of the grill until it is golden and cooked through but not too soft, about 5 minutes per side. If grilling the florets, cook them for an additional 4 or 5 minutes.

In a small bowl, stir together the tahini, lemon zest and juice, and ½ teaspoon each of salt and pepper. Add water 1 Tbsp at a time until the mixture is smooth and creamy. Taste and add more lemon juice and salt until the sauce tastes balanced between the nutty tahini and acid from the lemon.

Place the cauliflower on a platter, spoon the tahini sauce over, and sprinkle with the mint, parsley, cilantro, and green onion. Drizzle the pomegranate molasses over all. Serve immediately.

INDOOR METHOD: Preheat the oven to 400°F [200°C]. Heat a large cast-iron or other oven-proof skillet over medium-high heat. Slice the cauliflower as directed. Instead of oiling and seasoning the cauliflower, add 2 to 3 Tbsp oil to the pan. Once the oil is shimmering, cook the cauliflower steaks until deeply caramelized on both sides. Transfer the skillet to the oven and roast the steaks until deep brown and tender, but not too soft, about 10 minutes. Proceed with the remainder of the recipe as directed.

EGGPLANT ROLLATINI

This dish is fast, looks beautiful, and should be thought of as lasagna's lighter summer counterpart.

1 cup [240 g] ricotta cheese

½ cup [10 g] packed finely chopped fresh baby spinach

1 tsp lemon zest

¼ cup [15 g] grated pecorino romano cheese

Kosher salt

Freshly ground black pepper

1½ to 2 lbs [680 to 910 g] eggplant, cut lengthwise into ¼- to ½-in [6- to 12-mm] slices

3 Tbsp extra-virgin olive oil

One 14.5-oz [415-g] can crushed tomatoes

2 garlic cloves, thinly sliced

¼ tsp crushed red pepper flakes, plus more as needed

8 oz [230 g] shredded mozzarella

4 or 5 fresh basil leaves

Crusty bread, for serving

To prepare the filling: In a small bowl, stir together the ricotta cheese, spinach, lemon zest, pecorino cheese, a pinch of salt, and several grinds of pepper. Set aside.

Brush both sides of each eggplant slice with olive oil and season with salt and pepper. Heat the grill to medium-high and cook the eggplant until both sides have even grill marks and the vegetables are pliable but still very much intact, 2 to 3 minutes per side.

In a small bowl, mix the crushed tomatoes, garlic, red pepper flakes, 1 tsp salt, and a few grinds of pepper. Pour half of the tomato sauce on the bottom of an 8-by-8-in [20-by-20-cm]

baking dish. Divide the ricotta mixture among the eggplant slices (you can fill them one at a time, or lay them in a single layer on a baking sheet), placing a dollop at the wide end of each slice. Carefully roll up the eggplant around the filling. Line up the eggplant rolls in the baking dish on top of the tomato sauce, so they're nestled together. Spoon the rest of the tomato sauce over the rolls and top with the mozzarella cheese. Place the baking dish back on the grill for 12 to 15 minutes, covered, until the cheese is melted and the sauce is bubbling. Garnish with freshly torn basil leaves and serve with crusty bread.

The dish can be assembled, without the mozzarella cheese, up to two days before. Before serving, top with mozzarella, and finish cooking either on the grill or in a 450°F [230°C] oven for 15 to 20 minutes until the sauce is bubbling, the dish is heated through, and the cheese is melted.

INDOOR METHOD: Prepare the filling, eggplant, and tomato sauce as directed. Heat a ridged grill pan over medium-high heat. When the pan is very hot, add the eggplant slices in one layer, taking care not to crowd them. Cook the eggplant, turning once, until both sides have grill marks and the slices are pliable. Lay the eggplant slices on a baking sheet, and assemble as directed above. Preheat the oven to 450°F [230°C]. Once the rollatini are fully assembled in the baking dish, sprinkle with cheese and cook for 15 to 20 minutes until the sauce is bubbling and the cheese is melted and starting to brown.

TOMATOES, BRASSICAS, SQUASH, AND LEAVES

EGGPLANT STEAKS WITH MISO

This dish is lush. The eggplant turns silky, while maintaining some bite, and the miso has all those lovely umami flavors. This dish is very miso forward, so choose light or dark depending on how intense you want that salty funk to be. It works well with large sturdy eggplants or any of the beautiful heirloom varieties that show up in farmers' markets.

1 lb [450 g] eggplant
2 Tbsp olive oil
Kosher salt
2 Tbsp miso paste
1 Tbsp vegetable oil
1 Tbsp mirin
2 green onions, white and light green parts, thinly sliced, for garnish

Cut the eggplant lengthwise into steaks 1 in [2.5 cm] thick, discarding the end pieces, or cut small eggplants, such as the long, slim Japanese ones, in half lengthwise. Brush both sides with olive oil and sprinkle with salt. Set aside.

In a small bowl, stir together the miso, vegetable oil, and mirin until well combined.

Over medium-high heat, grill the eggplant until it's nicely charred on one side, about 5 minutes. Flip the steaks and use a spoon to spread a thin layer of the miso paste mixture on the grilled side of each eggplant steak. Close the lid to the grill and cook for another 4 to 5 minutes.

Transfer to a platter or plates, garnish with green onions, and serve immediately.

INDOOR METHOD: Preheat the broiler. Prepare the eggplant slices and miso paste mixture as directed. Lay the eggplant slices flat on a foil- or parchment-lined baking sheet and broil them until they start to brown, about 5 minutes. Flip the steaks, and use a spoon to spread a thin layer of the miso paste mixture on the cooked side of each eggplant steak. Broil for 5 minutes more. Proceed with the remainder of the recipe as directed.

TOMATOES, BRASSICAS, SQUASH, AND LEAVES

EGGPLANT SANDWICHES WITH PICKLES AND HARD-BOILED EGGS

Don't be put off by all of the components in this sandwich inspired by the Israeli *sabich*. Don't want to make your own hummus? No big deal; use store-bought. No pita? Pile all the components on some crusty grilled bread. Not into eggs? Skip them; we won't tell. Just try to get a good mix of flavors and textures.

4 large eggs

2 plum tomatoes, diced

1 Persian cucumber or ½ English cucumber [about 180 g], diced

1 jalapeño chile, minced

2 Tbsp finely chopped flat-leaf parsley

Juice of ½ lemon

3 Tbsp extra-virgin olive oil

Kosher salt

Freshly ground black pepper

2 small or 1 large eggplant, cut crosswise into ½-in [12-mm] thick rounds

4 sturdy pita breads

Smoky Eggplant Dip (page 28) or store-bought baba ghanoush

Charred Beet Hummus (page 24) or store-bought hummus

8 cornichons, thinly sliced

In a small saucepan, cover the eggs with cold water. Bring the water to a boil, let it boil for one minute, and then turn off the heat and let the eggs sit for 12 minutes. After 12 minutes, transfer the eggs to an ice bath or run them under cold water until they are cool enough to handle.

To prepare the cucumber and tomato salad: In a small bowl, combine the tomatoes, cucumber, jalapeño, parsley, lemon juice, 1 Tbsp olive oil, a pinch of salt, and a few grinds of black pepper. Set aside.

To prepare the eggplant: Brush both sides of each eggplant slice with the remaining 2 Tbsp of olive oil and season generously with kosher salt. Heat the grill to medium and cook the eggplant until each slice has pronounced grill marks and is cooked through, about 2 minutes per side. While you're grilling the eggplant, lightly toast the pita breads on the grill, about 30 seconds per side.

To assemble the sandwiches: Cut a slit at the top of each pita round. Then, working carefully so the pita doesn't tear, spread the eggplant dip on one side of the inside of the pocket and the beet hummus on the other. Divide the eggplant slices among pitas. Peel and cut the eggs into thin slices and lay them on top of the eggplant. Divide the cucumber and tomato salad among the pitas, along with the sliced cornichons. Serve immediately with extra napkins.

All of the components of this dish can be made earlier in the day, like the eggplant and salad, or up to a few days before, like the hummus, eggplant spread, and eggs. Just assemble at the last minute.

INDOOR METHOD: Prepare the eggs, cucumber and tomato salad, and eggplant as directed. Heat a ridged grill pan over medium-high heat. Cook the eggplant in batches. When the pan is very hot, add the eggplant slices in one layer, taking care not to crowd them. Cook the eggplant, turning once, until both sides have grill marks and the slices are cooked through. Transfer the eggplant to a plate and repeat with the remaining eggplant slices. Proceed with the remainder of the recipe as directed.

RATATOUILLE

This ratatouille is summery, light, and just a little bit fancy. It's also very simple—a good place to showcase those gorgeous farmers' market veggies—so season, season, season. Serve it with orzo on the side or piled on grilled crusty bread.

1 lb [455 g] eggplant, cut into
   ¼-in [6-mm] rounds

½ lb [225 g] zucchini (1 or 2), cut into
   ¼-in [6-mm] rounds

½ lb [225 g] yellow squash, cut into
   ¼-in [6-mm] rounds

2 red bell peppers, seeded, deribbed,
   and cut into very thin rings

6 Tbsp [90 ml] extra-virgin olive oil

Kosher salt

Freshly ground black pepper

½ red onion, cut into ¼-in [6 mm] rounds,
   keeping rings as intact as possible

¾ cup [180 ml] tomato purée

3 garlic cloves, thinly sliced

4 sprigs fresh oregano

6 oz [170 g] feta cheese

Finely chopped flat-leaf parsley, for garnish

Heat the grill to medium. Place the eggplant, zucchini, squash, and bell peppers in an 8-by-8-in [20-by-20-cm] baking dish or 10-in [25-cm] cast-iron skillet. Toss the vegetables with 3 Tbsp of oil and season liberally with salt and pepper. Brush the onion slices with 1 Tbsp oil and season with salt. Transfer all vegetables to the grill. Cook until they take on grill marks and just start to soften, 3 to 4 minutes, and then flip and cook for another 2 minutes.

While the vegetables are grilling, pour the tomato purée into the bottom of the same baking dish that was holding the vegetables, as it should still have a bit of oil and salt left behind. Season the purée with additional salt and pepper. Add the garlic and the leaves from 2 of the oregano sprigs. Stir to evenly distribute the garlic and herbs. Set aside.

Once the vegetables have grill marks on both sides, transfer them to a plate. To assemble the ratatouille, in the baking dish, make a layer of eggplant on top of the tomato purée, overlapping the slices slightly. Follow with a layer of zucchini, then a layer of onions, then peppers, then squash. If you have more vegetables, start again with the eggplant and repeat until all of the vegetables are used up. Press down lightly to compress the vegetables, drizzle with the remaining 2 Tbsp olive oil, the leaves from the two remaining oregano sprigs, and another sprinkling of salt and pepper. Crumble the feta over the top.

CONTINUED

Place the baking dish back on the grill and cover. Cook the ratatouille, undisturbed, for 10 to 15 minutes, until the sauce is bubbling and starting to caramelize at the edges of the pan, the vegetables are fully soft, and the feta is melted. Remove from the grill and sprinkle with the parsley. To serve, cut the ratatouille into squares, so the different layers are visible from the side.

INDOOR METHOD: Oil and season the vegetables as directed. Heat a ridged grill pan over medium-high heat. When the pan is very hot, add the eggplant, zucchini, squash, bell pepper, and onion slices in batches, taking care not to crowd them together. Cook each vegetable, turning once, until both sides have grill marks and are just starting to soften. As the vegetables finish cooking, transfer them to a plate, and then layer as directed above. Preheat the oven to 400°F [200°C]. Once the ratatouille is fully assembled, transfer the cast-iron skillet or baking dish to the oven and bake for 10 to 15 minutes until the sauce is bubbling and starting to caramelize at the edges of the pan, the vegetables are fully soft, and the feta is melted. Serve as directed.

ZUCCHINI TARTINES WITH GOAT CHEESE AND PICKLED CARROTS

This is the zucchini recipe for people who don't really like zucchini. Like all sandwiches, it's customizable, and it has a ton of flavor. Swap eggplant for the zucchini, pickled radishes for the carrots, or feta for the goat cheese. You could skip the basil oil and use plain olive oil, but you shouldn't; the basil flavor really elevates the dish.

2 small zucchini, cut into rectangular slices ½ in [12 mm] thick and 2 to 3 in [5 to 7.5 cm] long

1 tsp kosher salt, plus more for sprinkling

½ cup [120 ml] Basil Oil (page 31)

4 slices crusty bread, each cut 1 in [2.5 cm] thick

2 Tbsp extra-virgin olive oil

4 oz [110 g] goat cheese

Pickled Carrots (page 30), with carrots cut into rectangular planks

Flaky salt, such as Maldon, for finishing

In a shallow bowl, toss the zucchini with 1 tsp kosher salt and then mix gently with the basil oil, so all pieces are coated. Let sit for at least 30 minutes and up to 4 hours at room temperature. Heat your grill to medium and cook the zucchini until it has caramelized and has grill marks, 2 to 3 minutes per side. Reserve any basil oil left in the bowl.

Brush both sides of the bread slices with olive oil and sprinkle lightly with salt. Grill over medium heat until both sides are golden and toasted, about 4 minutes total.

To assemble the sandwiches, divide the goat cheese among the bread slices, spreading the cheese to the edges. Top with as many zucchini slices as will fit across. Lay carrot slices on top of the zucchini, and drizzle each tartine with the reserved basil oil. Finish with a sprinkle of flaky salt.

INDOOR METHOD: Prepare the zucchini as directed. Heat a ridged grill pan over medium-high heat. When the pan is very hot, add the zucchini slices in one layer, taking care not to crowd them. Cook the zucchini, turning once, until both sides have caramelized and the slices are cooked through. Transfer the zucchini to a plate and repeat with the remaining slices until it is all cooked. Toast the bread as directed on page 36 and then assemble the sandwiches as directed above.

MOROCCAN-SPICED SQUASH FATTOUSH WITH LENTILS

This salad is loosely based on a more traditional Lebanese fattoush. It has the grilled pita and fresh veggies but takes a tour through Morocco, picking up those warm, sweet spices. If you can't find Halloumi, substitute another salty cheese, such as feta, and add it fresh to the mix.

½ cup [100 g] French Puy or Beluga lentils

2 tsp ground sumac

1 Tbsp pomegranate molasses

2 tsp white wine vinegar

Juice from ½ lemon, about 2 Tbsp

½ cup [120 ml] extra-virgin olive oil, plus more as needed

1 tsp kosher salt, plus more as needed

1 lb [450 g] delicata or butternut squash, cut into 1-in [2.5-cm] pieces

1 small garlic clove, minced

¼ tsp ground cumin

¼ tsp ground coriander

½ tsp ground cinnamon

Pinch of cayenne pepper

5 to 6 oz [140 to 170 g] Halloumi cheese, cut into 1-in [2.5-cm] cubes

Two 8-in [20-cm] pita rounds

1 cup [150 g] finely diced English or Persian cucumber

6 dates, pitted and chopped

1 small or ½ large fennel bulb, about 8 oz [230 g], finely chopped

½ cup [20 g] chopped fresh mint leaves

Freshly ground black pepper

¼ cup [55 g] tahini

Cook the lentils as directed on the package, taking care not to overcook them so they keep their shape.

Make the dressing: In a small bowl, soak the sumac in 2 tsp warm water for 10 minutes. Add the pomegranate molasses, vinegar, and lemon juice and stir to combine. Whisk in ¼ cup olive oil and season with salt. Set aside.

In a large bowl, toss the squash with the remaining ¼ cup oil and garlic. In a small bowl or jar, combine the cumin, coriander, cinnamon, cayenne, and 1 tsp kosher salt. Sprinkle the spice mixture over the squash, tossing again, so the pieces are evenly coated.

In a small bowl, toss the Halloumi cubes with enough oil to coat.

Brush each pita lightly with olive oil. Heat the grill to medium-high and top with a mesh grill topper. Grill the squash on the topper, tossing occasionally, until it's well charred in spots and tender, about 15 minutes. At the same time, grill the Halloumi, tossing occasionally, until it has grill marks on all sides and is beginning to melt, about 2 minutes total. Grill the pita on both sides until it's golden and crisp, with grill marks, about 3 minutes per side. When cool enough to handle, break the pita into bite-size pieces.

In a large bowl, combine the squash, Halloumi, cucumber, dates, fennel, mint, and pita pieces and toss gently. Add the dressing and toss again to coat. Check the seasoning and drizzle the tahini over all. Serve immediately.

INDOOR METHOD: Prepare the lentils and dressing as directed. Preheat the oven to 400°F [200°C]. On a foil- or parchment-lined baking sheet, oil and season the squash as directed. Roast until tender and caramelized, 15 to 20 minutes. At the same time, toast the pita directly on the oven rack until crisp at the edges and slightly golden. Heat a cast-iron skillet over medium heat. Instead of tossing the Halloumi with oil, pat it very dry with paper towels. Add 2 Tbsp oil to the skillet. When the oil is shimmering, fry the cheese until all sides are golden brown. Proceed with the remainder of the recipe as directed.

COCONUT CURRY SQUASH

Marinating the squash for this recipe in the sauce ensures that each slice fully absorbs all of the vibrant flavors of ginger, garlic, turmeric, and coconut. Not only does this dish look gorgeous, but first marinating and then grilling the squash makes it feel almost meaty.

2 cups [400 g] long-grain rice, such as jasmine or basmati

1 stalk lemongrass, or 1 tsp packed lime zest

4 garlic cloves

One 2-in [5-cm] piece fresh ginger, peeled and coarsely chopped

1 shallot, peeled and coarsely chopped

½ tsp crushed red pepper flakes, plus more as needed

1 tsp ground turmeric

1 tsp kosher salt, plus more as needed

3 Tbsp vegetable oil

One 3-in [7.5-cm] cinnamon stick

4 cardamom pods, slightly crushed

2 star anise pods

One 13.5-oz [400-ml] can unsweetened coconut milk

1 kabocha or acorn squash, stem and seeds removed, cut into ½-in [12-mm] half-moon slices

Finely chopped fresh cilantro, for garnish

Fried Shallots (optional, page 33)

Crushed salted peanuts, for garnish

Prepare the rice as directed on the package.

Peel off and discard the tough outer layers of the lemongrass and finely grate the bottom 3 in [7.5 cm] of the stalk. In the bowl of a blender or food processor, combine the grated lemongrass, garlic, ginger, shallot, ½ tsp crushed red pepper, turmeric, and 1 tsp salt with ¼ cup [60 ml] water. Pulse until it forms a paste. In a large shallow pan (large enough to hold all of the squash), heat 1 Tbsp vegetable oil over medium-high heat. Fry the spice paste until the water evaporates and it begins to brown and stick to the pan, about 5 minutes. Add the remaining lemongrass stalk, cinnamon, cardamom, star anise, and coconut milk. Bring to a boil, turn the heat down to the lowest it will go, and simmer for 6 to 7 minutes. Remove from the heat, add the squash slices to the hot curry sauce, and let sit for at least 1 hour and up to 4 hours at room temperature.

Heat the grill to medium-high. Grill the squash slices, shaking off any extra sauce, until caramelized on both sides and tender, about 10 minutes total. Meanwhile, rewarm the sauce on the grill. When the squash slices are done, return them to the sauce.

Divide the rice among four bowls or heap onto a serving platter. Top the rice with the grilled squash slices, pour the sauce over all, and garnish with cilantro, fried shallots, if using, and peanuts.

INDOOR METHOD: Prepare the rice, sauce, and squash as directed. After the squash has marinated, sear it in a ridged grill pan or cast-iron skillet over medium-high heat until the exterior is caramelized, and it's tender all the way through, covering the pan with a lid, if necessary. Continue with the remainder of the recipe as directed.

SQUASH TACOS WITH BLACK BEANS, PICKLED ONIONS, AND PEPITA SALSA

Like all good tacos, this version, made with butternut squash, is full of flavor, color, and texture. Be sure to make the pickles, as their crunchy, salty bite brings out the best of the sweet squash.

One 15-oz [425-g] can black beans

½ tsp dried oregano

1½ tsp kosher salt

¼ small red onion, finely chopped

1½ lbs [680 g] butternut squash, peeled and cut into 1-in [2.5-cm] cubes, or yellow and green summer squash, cut into wide strips

3 Tbsp extra-virgin olive oil

¼ tsp cumin

¼ tsp chili powder

8 corn tortillas

Pepita Salsa (recipe follows)

Pickles Two Ways (page 30; use red onions and radishes)

Cilantro leaves, for garnish

Drain and rinse the beans and then add them to a small pot with the oregano, ½ tsp of salt, the red onion, and ¼ cup [60 ml] water. Bring to a simmer and cook 10 to 15 minutes until the beans are slightly thickened and the flavors have melded, but the beans are still fully intact. Keep warm.

In a large bowl, toss the squash with the oil, 1 tsp salt, cumin, and chili powder. If using a charcoal grill, make a medium-hot fire; otherwise heat a gas grill to high. Using a grill topper, cook the squash cubes over the hottest part of the grill and turn until they have grill marks on all sides and are a bit charred at the edges, 2 to 3 minutes per side. Once the squash has taken on color, move the whole grill topper to the cool part of the grill, cover, and cook until the pieces are tender but still offer some resistance when pierced with a knife, 8 to 10 minutes more. Remove from the grill.

Lightly grill the tortillas on the coolest part of the grill. When they're heated through and soft, wrap them in a clean kitchen towel to transport them to the table. To assemble the tacos, top each tortilla with pepita salsa, squash, beans, and pickled onions and radishes. Garnish with cilantro leaves and serve immediately.

INDOOR METHOD: Prepare the beans as directed. Preheat the oven to 400°F [200°C]. On a foil- or parchment-lined baking sheet, oil and season the squash as directed. Roast until tender and caramelized, 15 to 20 minutes. Proceed with the remainder of the recipe as directed, using a dry medium skillet, or the microwave, to heat the tortillas before serving.

CONTINUED

PEPITA SALSA

Adding pumpkin seeds to the salsa adds a nice texture to the Squash Tacos. This salsa is also great in a bowl with tortilla chips or spread on a quesadilla before grilling.

3 medium tomatoes, coarsely chopped

½ cup [70 g] roasted, salted pepitas or shelled pumpkin seeds, toasted

2 Tbsp chopped red onion

1 canned chipotle chile in adobo sauce, plus 1 Tbsp adobo sauce

2 Tbsp chopped cilantro

1 small garlic clove

1 tsp kosher salt

Freshly ground black pepper

In a blender or food processor, combine the tomatoes, pepitas, onion, chipotle, adobo sauce, cilantro, and garlic clove and blend until the mixture is well combined but still has texture. Taste and adjust seasoning.

TOFU TACOS WITH CREAMY CABBAGE SLAW

These tacos hit all the right taco notes—heat from the taco seasoning (it takes 5 minutes to make and is so much better than Old El Paso); cool, creamy, crunchy slaw, with depth from the chile; extra texture from the pepitas; and the bite of salty cotija cheese. Just add some Coronas with lime.

14 oz [400 g] extra-firm tofu
2 Tbsp chili powder
1½ tsp ground cumin
2 tsp cornstarch
2 tsp kosher salt
1½ tsp smoked paprika
1 tsp ground coriander
2 Tbsp extra-virgin olive oil
8 corn tortillas
Creamy Chipotle Slaw (recipe follows)
Cotija cheese, crumbled
Toasted pepitas (pumpkin seeds), sliced
    avocado, chopped cilantro, and
    lime wedges, for garnish (optional)

On a plate, cutting board, or baking sheet, wrap the tofu in several layers of paper towels. Place another plate or baking sheet on top and weigh down with books, cans, or something else heavy to remove as much moisture as possible. Let sit for at least half an hour or up to 6 hours—the longer the better.

To make the taco seasoning: In a small jar, combine the chili powder, cumin, cornstarch, salt, paprika, and coriander. Shake and set aside.

Meanwhile, preheat the grill to medium. Unwrap the tofu and cut each block into ½-in [12-mm] slices. Generously season both sides of each tofu slice with the taco seasoning and brush with the oil. Grill, oiled-side down, for 3 or 4 minutes until grill marks show and the tofu is heated through. Oil the other side and flip each slice. Grill 3 or 4 minutes more. When the tofu is done, transfer to a plate and cut each plank into strips ½ in [12 mm] wide.

Grill the tortillas over medium heat until warm, with slight char marks, 30 seconds or so per side. To assemble each taco, add tofu strips to a tortilla, pile on the chipotle slaw, and garnish with crumbled cotija cheese. Top with additional garnishes such as pepitas, avocado, cilantro, or a squeeze of lime juice. Serve immediately.

INDOOR METHOD: Prepare the taco seasoning. Ready the tofu to the point of seasoning the slices but skip brushing the tofu with oil. Instead add the 2 Tbsp oil to a cast-iron or other skillet over medium heat. When the oil is shimmering, add the tofu slices. Cook the tofu until crisp and golden on both sides and warmed all the way through. Transfer to a plate. Wipe out the skillet, lower the heat to medium, and heat the tortillas one at a time until they are warm and brown in spots. Transfer the tortillas to a plate and cover them with a clean kitchen towel. Alternatively, heat all of the tortillas at once on a microwave-safe plate, covered by a damp paper towel. Assemble the tacos as directed.

CREAMY
CHIPOTLE SLAW

½ cup [120 g] plain Greek yogurt
1 canned chipotle in adobo, finely chopped,
   plus 1 Tbsp adobo sauce
Juice of 1 lime
½ tsp sugar
¼ tsp ground cumin
Kosher salt
1 small head of purple or green cabbage,
   shredded
5 radishes, thinly sliced
3 Tbsp chopped cilantro
2 Tbsp thinly sliced red onion

In a small bowl, stir together the yogurt, adobo
sauce, chipotle, lime juice, sugar, cumin, a pinch
of kosher salt, and 1 tsp water.

In a medium bowl, combine the cabbage, radishes, cilantro, and red onion and toss with the
yogurt-chipotle dressing until all of the vegetables are evenly coated. Taste for seasoning.

RED CABBAGE WITH PEANUT DRESSING AND GRILLED PINEAPPLE

This recipe looks beautiful with its golden pineapple and vibrant purple cabbage. A salt cure makes the dense cabbage more supple, and all of that salinity balances out the sweetness of the fruit. And grill the unused portion of the pineapple (the recipe calls for only half), unseasoned, and serve it with scoops of vanilla ice cream and some toasted coconut flakes for dessert.

½ head of red cabbage

¼ cup [60 ml] extra-virgin olive oil

Kosher salt

½ medium pineapple (about 3½ lbs [1.6 kg] whole, or 1 lb [455 g] pieces once trimmed)

Spicy Peanut Dressing (recipe follows)

½ cup [70 g] salted peanuts, toasted and coarsely chopped

3 Tbsp finely chopped fresh cilantro, for garnish

Cut the cabbage in half and cut the half into 1- to 2-in [2.5- to 5-cm] wedges, leaving the core as intact as possible to help the wedges stay together. Drizzle the cabbage with oil until well coated and sprinkle generously with salt. Let the cabbage sit for at least 1 hour and up to 6 hours to let it cure.

Heat your grill to medium. Cut the top and bottom off of the pineapple and discard. Standing the pineapple up tall, use a sharp knife to cut around the fruit to remove the skin. Discard the outside. Cut the pineapple in half lengthwise. Set aside one half and cut the other half into 1- to 2-in [2.5- to 5-cm] spears, removing the tough core at the center. Brush the pineapple spears with oil.

Grill both the cabbage and the pineapple over medium heat until the pineapple has become deeply caramelized and the cabbage has grill marks and outer edges that have started to char, about 5 minutes for the cabbage and 10 minutes for the pineapple.

Transfer the cabbage and pineapple to a platter. Drizzle generously with the dressing, sprinkle with peanuts, garnish with cilantro, and serve immediately.

INDOOR METHOD: Heat a ridged grill pan or cast-iron skillet over medium-high heat. Prepare the cabbage and pineapple as directed. When the pan is hot, add the cabbage in a single layer (this may take two batches) and cook, until the edges are well charred and the wedges are cooked through. Transfer the cabbage to a platter and add the pineapple to the grill pan, cooking until it's deeply caramelized. Proceed as directed.

CONTINUED

SPICY PEANUT DRESSING

This addictive peanut dressing is slightly adapted from the one that the lovely Jenny Rosenstrach includes on her blog, *Dinner: A Love Story*. It's rich from the peanut butter, a little spicy, and not quite as thick as the Peanut Dipping Sauce (page 115) included in this book. It's so delicious that you might just try to put it on every salad from here on out.

⅓ cup [85 g] peanut butter (creamy or crunchy)
⅓ cup [80 ml] rice wine vinegar
2 Tbsp soy sauce
1 tsp maple syrup
1 tsp hot sauce
1 garlic clove, peeled and finely grated
1 tsp fresh ginger, peeled and finely grated

In a small bowl or measuring cup, stir together the peanut butter, vinegar, soy sauce, maple syrup, hot sauce, garlic, and ginger until well combined. If the dressing is too thick, thin with warm water, 1 tsp at a time, until it's pourable. The dressing will keep, refrigerated, for up to 4 days.

BRUSSELS SPROUTS WITH HERBS AND FRIED SHALLOTS

The Brussels sprouts that David Chang serves at Momofuku Ssäm Bar in New York inspire this dish. While it loses the puffed rice and fried cilantro leaves (why would you fry cilantro if you could fry shallots instead?), it captures that same funky, sweet, smoky flavor.

1 lb [455 g] Brussels sprouts, trimmed and halved

3 Tbsp vegetable oil

Kosher salt

Fish Sauce Vinaigrette (recipe follows)

Fried Shallots (page 33)

3 Tbsp finely chopped fresh mint

3 Tbsp finely chopped fresh cilantro

Trim and halve the Brussels sprouts, discarding any loose or shriveled leaves. In a large bowl, toss with the vegetable oil and season with salt. Heat your grill to medium-high and top with a mesh grill topper. Cook the sprouts until they are evenly charred and tender but not at all mushy, about 6 minutes total, flipping once halfway through.

When the sprouts are done, transfer to a bowl (the one you used earlier is fine), toss with the vinaigrette, and liberally garnish with shallots and herbs. Serve immediately.

INDOOR METHOD: Preheat the broiler. Trim, oil, and season the Brussels sprouts as directed. On a foil-lined baking sheet, broil the sprouts, tossing a few times, until they are well charred in spots and tender, 8 to 10 minutes.

FISH SAUCE VINAIGRETTE

This dressing is a little bit funky and sweet; it works great with this recipe, as well as with grilled broccoli or cauliflower. It would also be a good alternative dipping sauce for the Mushroom and Tofu Spring Rolls (page 114).

¼ cup [60 ml] fish sauce

¼ cup [60 ml] water

¼ cup [60 ml] maple syrup

1 small red chile, minced

1 small garlic clove, minced

In a small bowl or directly into a measuring cup, stir together the fish sauce, water, maple syrup, chile, and garlic. This sauce keeps, refrigerated, for 3 days.

SERVES 4

RADICCHIO SALAD WITH ORANGES AND PECORINO

The radicchio is quite bitter, but its bite plays well with the funky anchovies, salty cheese, and sweet orange. When stone fruit is in season, swap out the oranges for lightly grilled sliced plums or peaches.

1 large head of radicchio
1 navel orange
Anchovy Red Wine Vinaigrette (recipe follows)
2 oz [60 g] pecorino romano cheese
2 Tbsp chopped fresh mint leaves
¼ cup [30 g] pistachios, coarsely chopped

Remove any loose outer leaves from the radicchio. Cut the head in half through the stem end, cut each half in half, and then cut each quarter in half again. You will have 8 wedges.

To prepare the orange, slice off both ends. Using a sharp knife and slicing downward, remove the peel and white pith and discard. Working over a bowl to catch the juice, cut the segments from the membranes separating them and discard the membranes. Set aside.

Arrange the radicchio in a single layer and drizzle both sides of each wedge with some of the vinaigrette, using 2 Tbsp total. If using a charcoal grill, let the fire die down to medium heat, or heat a gas grill to medium. Grill each wedge until the edges are charred and the radicchio is warm and slightly wilted, 1 to 2 minutes per side.

To assemble, arrange the radicchio wedges on a platter. Drizzle with half of the remaining dressing and then scatter the orange segments on top. Using a vegetable peeler, shave slices of pecorino on top. Sprinkle mint and pistachios over all. Add more dressing if desired. Serve immediately, passing extra dressing at the table.

INDOOR METHOD: Heat a ridged grill pan or cast-iron skillet over medium-high heat. Prepare the radicchio and the orange as directed. When the pan is hot, add the lettuce in a single layer (this may take a few batches), cut-side down, and cook until the edges are well charred and the wedges are cooked through. Transfer the radicchio to a platter and proceed as directed.

CONTINUED

ANCHOVY RED WINE VINAIGRETTE

2 anchovy fillets, minced
1 small garlic clove, minced
½ tsp kosher salt
¼ cup [60 ml] red wine vinegar
¼ cup [60 ml] extra-virgin olive oil
¼ tsp freshly ground black pepper

Using a mortar and pestle or a chef's knife, smash or chop the anchovies, garlic, and salt until they form a paste. Transfer to a small bowl or jar; add the vinegar, olive oil, and pepper and stir well, or shake vigorously until well combined. Set the dressing aside. It can be made a day or two in advance, but be aware that the garlic and anchovy flavors will become more pronounced as the mixture sits.

CHICORIES WITH ANCHOVY VINAIGRETTE AND EGGS

This salad has plenty of umami flavors from the anchovies and cheese, which play well with the bitter sweetness from the chicories. Want to make it even more substantial? Add a handful of Grilled Croutons (page 37), Charred Chickpeas (page 34), or both.

2 anchovy fillets

1 small garlic clove

½ tsp kosher salt, plus more as needed

½ tsp Dijon mustard

¼ cup [60 ml] red wine vinegar

¼ cup [60 ml] extra-virgin olive oil, plus more for brushing

Freshly ground black pepper

4 eggs

2 or 3 heads of chicories, such as radicchio, endive, Treviso, etc.

¼ cup [10 g] finely chopped flat-leaf parsley

Flaky salt, such as Maldon, for finishing

2 oz [60 g] Manchego cheese

Using a mortar and pestle or a chef's knife, smash or chop the anchovies, garlic, and ½ tsp salt until they form a paste. Transfer to a small bowl or jar; add the mustard, vinegar, ¼ cup [60 ml] of the olive oil, and pepper and stir well, or shake vigorously until well combined. Set the dressing aside. It can be made a day or two in advance, but keep in mind that the garlic and anchovy flavors will bloom and become more pronounced as the dressing sits.

Fill a small saucepan with water and bring to a boil. Turning the heat down so that it barely simmers, gently lower the eggs into the water and cook for exactly 6 minutes. Transfer the eggs to an ice bath or run under cold water to stop cooking. Set aside to cool.

Cut the chicories in half or in quarters, depending on the size of the head, keeping the stem ends intact so the sections hold together. Brush the cut sides with olive oil and sprinkle with salt. Heat your grill to medium and grill the chicories, cut-side down, until the edges begin to char and crisp and the leaves wilt slightly, 1 to 2 minutes. Transfer to a cutting board and coarsely chop. In a bowl, toss the grilled chicories with a few tablespoons of the dressing (you won't use it all) and the parsley.

Divide the salad among four plates. Carefully peel the eggs and nestle one on top of each salad. Season each egg with a pinch of flaky salt and freshly ground pepper. Using a vegetable peeler, garnish each salad with several thin strips of Manchego. Serve immediately.

INDOOR METHOD: Prepare the dressing and eggs as directed. Heat a ridged grill pan or cast-iron skillet over medium-high heat and then prepare the chicories as directed. When the pan is hot, add the lettuce in a single layer (this may take a few batches), cut-side down, and cook until the edges are well charred and the wedges are cooked through. Transfer the chicories to plates and proceed as directed.

TOMATOES, BRASSICAS, SQUASH, AND LEAVES

KALE CHIPS WITH GRILLED ONION DIP

This onion dip is a really, really good version of a classic. It goes very well with these kale chips, but it is equally at home with potato chips or carrot and celery sticks.

2 medium yellow or red onions, cut into ¾-in [2-cm] slices
Extra-virgin olive oil
1½ cups [360 g] plain, full-fat Greek yogurt
½ cup [120 g] mayonnaise
1 tsp garlic powder
2 tsp kosher salt, plus more
2 green onions, thinly sliced
1 big bunch of lacinato or dino kale

Heat the grill to medium. Brush both sides of each onion slice with oil. Grill until the onion slices are well charred and softened, about 5 minutes per side. Meanwhile, in a medium bowl, stir together the yogurt, mayonnaise, garlic powder, 2 tsp salt, and green onions until well combined. When the grilled onions are done, transfer to a cutting board and let cool slightly. When they are cool enough to handle, finely chop them, add to the dip mixture, and stir to evenly distribute them through the dip. Check for seasoning and set aside.

Reduce the heat of the grill to medium-low. Trim the toughest ends off the kale. Lay the kale leaves on a baking sheet and brush with olive oil until each leaf is coated. Sprinkle generously with salt. Grill in a single layer until the leaves are crisp, watching carefully so that they don't char too much, about 2 minutes per side.

Serve the kale chips with the onion dip. The dip can be made several hours ahead of time; refrigerate until ready to use.

INDOOR METHOD: Preheat your broiler. Lay out the onion slices on a foil-lined baking sheet and brush both sides with oil. Broil the onions, flipping once, until they are brown on both sides and cooked through, 10 to 15 minutes total. Prepare the onion dip as directed. Turn the oven to bake at 350°F [180°C]. Trim the kale as directed, and on two foil- or parchment-lined baking sheets, brush both sides of each kale leaf with oil and season with salt. Bake until the chips are crisp and their edges are brown, but not burned, 10 to 15 minutes. Serve as directed.

CAESAR WITH GRILLED CROUTONS

Grilling romaine gives it an almost nutty taste. You can make the dressing by hand, or a small food processor will do the job in a snap. No need to chop the anchovies first.

4 anchovy fillets packed in oil, drained and finely chopped

1 egg yolk

Finely grated zest and juice from 1 lemon

1 tsp Dijon mustard

1 small garlic clove, finely minced or grated

1½ tsp kosher salt, plus more as needed

Freshly ground black pepper

¼ cup [60 ml] vegetable oil

⅓ cup [80 ml] extra-virgin olive oil

⅓ cup [10 g] finely grated Parmesan cheese, plus more for serving

3 slices crusty bread, each cut 1 in [2.5 cm] thick

2 hearts of romaine lettuce

In a medium bowl, stir together the anchovies, egg yolk, lemon zest and juice, mustard, garlic, 1½ tsp of salt, and pepper. Very slowly add the vegetable oil and 2 Tbsp of olive oil, first adding one drop at a time and then moving to a thin steady stream, whisking constantly until the ingredients are all incorporated and you have a smooth, creamy dressing. Stir in the Parmesan cheese. You can also make the Caesar dressing in a food processor.

Heat your grill to medium. Cut the bread slices into ½-in [12-mm] cubes and toss with 2 Tbsp of olive oil, squeezing the bread so it absorbs as much oil as possible. Season lightly with salt. Then, using a mesh grill topper, grill the croutons until they're golden and crisp, tossing occasionally, 4 to 5 minutes. Set aside.

Cut the romaine hearts in half lengthwise, keeping the stems intact. Drizzle the cut side with the remaining 2 Tbsp of olive oil and sprinkle with salt. Over medium heat, grill the romaine hearts until the edges begin to crisp and the lettuce takes on char marks, 1 to 2 minutes per side.

To assemble, put one romaine heart half on each plate. Drizzle generously with Caesar dressing, and divide the croutons among the plates. Finish with more grated Parmesan, if desired, and freshly ground pepper. Serve immediately.

INDOOR METHOD: Make the dressing and croutons as directed. Heat a ridged grill pan or cast-iron skillet over medium-high heat and prepare the romaine for cooking as directed. When the pan is hot, add the lettuce in a single layer (this may take two batches), cut-side down, and cook until the edges are well charred and the wedges are slightly wilted. Transfer the romaine to plates and proceed as directed.

GREEN VEGETABLES, PEAS, BEANS, AND GRAINS

ASPARAGUS AND GREEN BEANS WITH FARRO, PEAS, AND RICOTTA SALATA

This salad is my most requested recipe. It's great for a party, makes terrific leftovers, and is endlessly adaptable. Swap all of the green veggies for grilled plums, carrots, and toasted almonds in the fall, or shredded kale, hazelnuts, and roasted parsnips in the winter. It also can be made in advance; just add the mint and cheese at the last minute.

1 cup [180 g] uncooked farro

3 Tbsp finely chopped red onion

¼ cup [60 ml] apple cider vinegar

1 tsp kosher salt, plus more as needed

⅓ cup [80 ml] extra-virgin olive oil, plus more as needed

1 small bunch of asparagus

6 oz [175 g] green beans, trimmed

6 oz [175 g] sugar snap peas, trimmed

6 radishes, thinly sliced

½ cup [60 g] frozen peas, thawed

½ cup [20 g] finely chopped fresh mint

½ cup [about 40 g] ricotta salata, or other salty cheese such as feta or cotija

Freshly ground black pepper

Cook the farro according to the package directions.

In a large bowl, combine the onion, vinegar, and salt and let stand as you prepare all of the other vegetables, or at least 10 minutes. Then add ⅓ cup [80 ml] of the oil and whisk to combine. Set the dressing aside.

Snap the tough ends off the asparagus. Toss the asparagus, green beans, and sugar snap peas with a few tablespoons of olive oil and sprinkle with salt.

Heat your grill to medium-high. Use a grill topper for the beans and sugar snaps and cook the asparagus, beans, and sugar snap peas, tossing and turning occasionally until all are charred in spots and crisp-tender, 4 to 5 minutes. Remove from the grill and let cool slightly.

When the grilled vegetables are cool enough to handle, cut into pieces 1 in [2.5 cm] long and add them to the bowl with the dressing along with the farro, radishes, thawed peas, mint, and cheese. Toss well and taste for salt and pepper. Serve immediately or later at room temperature. The salad can be made up to two days in advance. Keep refrigerated and add the mint and cheese just before serving.

INDOOR METHOD: Prepare the farro and dressing as directed. While preheating the broiler, also prepare the asparagus, green beans, and sugar snap peas as directed. On a foil-lined rimmed baking sheet, broil those vegetables until charred and blistered in spots and cooked through, about 6 minutes. Continue as directed.

ASPARAGUS WITH FRIED EGGS AND GARLIC CHIPS

Simply grilled, well-seasoned asparagus is a terrific side dish. (Those crispy tips!) This recipe takes the spring staple vegetable one step further by coating the asparagus in flavorful garlic oil and adding crispy garlic chips and lacy fried eggs.

8 garlic cloves, peeled and thinly sliced
¼ cup [60 ml] extra-virgin olive oil, plus 2 Tbsp
2 bunches of asparagus, tough ends trimmed
Kosher salt
1 tsp lemon zest
¼ tsp crushed red pepper flakes (optional)
4 eggs
Flaky salt, such as Maldon
Freshly ground black pepper
¼ cup [8 g] finely grated Parmesan cheese

In a medium skillet, combine the garlic and ¼ cup olive oil. Cook over medium-low heat, stirring often, until the garlic turns golden. Don't rush it; the low heat means maximum garlic flavor in the oil. Line a small plate with paper towels. Place the asparagus on a rimmed baking sheet.

Watch the garlic closely toward the end. When it is evenly toasted, use a fine mesh strainer to strain the garlic oil over the asparagus. Lay the garlic chips (left behind in the strainer) on the plate lined with paper towels and sprinkle with salt. Reserve the pan, returning it to the stove, leaving a light coating of garlic oil.

Toss the asparagus with the garlic oil until it's evenly coated and sprinkle generously with salt.

Heat the grill to medium-high and cook the asparagus until it's crisp-tender and charred in spots, with crispy tips. When the asparagus is done, while still hot, toss with the lemon zest and red pepper flakes, if using. Cover with foil to keep warm.

Heat the same skillet you used for the garlic over medium heat, adding an additional tablespoon of oil, if necessary. When the oil is shimmering and a drop of water immediately sizzles and evaporates, crack 2 eggs into opposite sides of the pan. Fry until the whites are crisp at the edges and underneath and set, keeping the yolks liquid. Carefully transfer the eggs to a plate and repeat with the remaining eggs, adding more oil if needed.

Divide the asparagus among four plates and top each pile of asparagus with an egg. Season each egg with flaky salt and freshly ground pepper, sprinkle Parmesan over all, and garnish with the garlic chips. Serve immediately.

INDOOR METHOD: Preheat the broiler. Prepare the garlic and asparagus with the garlic oil as above. On a foil-lined baking sheet, broil the asparagus until charred and blistered in spots and cooked through, about 7 minutes. Continue as directed.

ARTICHOKES WITH LEMON-CAPER AIOLI

Artichokes are jerks. They're full of poky thorns, and you can't even eat the whole thing. That said, they're incredibly delicious, and this is perhaps one of the simplest, most flavorful ways to prepare them. Rather than end up with a soggy, steamy vegetable, you will sit down to artichokes that are crisp and savory. The lemon-caper aioli is luxurious, but simple melted butter works well, too.

4 baby artichokes or 2 large globe artichokes
2 lemons, halved
3 to 4 Tbsp [45 to 60 ml] olive oil
Kosher salt
1 Tbsp capers, drained and finely chopped
1 Tbsp fresh tarragon, finely chopped
Classic Aioli and Variations (page 20)

If using baby artichokes: Trim off the outer leaves and slice each artichoke in half length-wise. Rub all of the cut sides with one of the lemon halves. In a bowl large enough for all of the artichokes, toss them with the olive oil and sprinkle with salt. Heat your grill to medium-high and grill, cut-side down first, until the artichokes are tender and charred. After about 5 minutes, flip and grill for another 5 minutes or so.

If using large globe artichokes: Prepare a bath for the vegetables by filling a large bowl (large enough to fit all of the artichokes) with cold water. Squeeze the juice from one lemon half into the water and add the rind. With a sharp knife, trim any brown parts off the stem of each artichoke. Next, cut off the top inch [2.5 cm] or so as well. Using scissors, remove any loose leaves on the outside of the artichokes and also trim off the prickly tips of all of the leaves, rubbing all the cut surfaces with lemon. Cut each artichoke in half lengthwise, keeping the pieces you're not working on in the prepared water bath. Using a small, sharp knife, carefully cut out the fuzzy choke from the middle of each artichoke half and discard. Let all 4 halves soak in the lemon-water bath for 10 minutes.

Heat the grill to medium-high and make an aluminum foil packet for the artichokes. Double over a very large sheet of heavy-duty aluminum foil so you have a 24-in [60-cm] square. You may have to make two packets if your artichokes are very large. Arrange the artichokes in a single layer in the middle of the foil, cut-side up. Discard the lemon water bath. Distribute ½ cup of fresh water among the cavities of the arti-chokes, season with salt, and drizzle with 3 to 4 Tbsp of olive oil. Carefully fold up the packets and crimp the edges so that they're fully sealed. Place the packets on the grill and cook for 10 to 15 minutes. Flip the packets and cook for 10 to 15 minutes more. Carefully open the packets. At this point, the tip of a sharp knife should easily pierce the artichoke heart. Place the artichokes directly on the grill, cut-side down, and grill for another 8 to 10 minutes until the artichokes are well charred.

CONTINUED

While the artichokes are grilling, stir the capers and tarragon into the aioli. As the artichokes finish grilling, transfer them to a plate. Serve the artichokes while still hot—or let them come to room temperature and then serve—with the aioli on the side.

INDOOR METHOD: Preheat the oven to 400°F [200°C]. Prepare the artichokes as directed, wrap them in a foil packet, and then put the packets on a baking sheet. Roast the artichokes in the packets for 45 minutes to 1 hour, flipping once halfway through. Pull the sheet from the oven and turn on the broiler. Carefully open the packets (the steam will be hot!) and test for doneness. The leaves should pull away easily, and the tip of a sharp knife should slip through the artichoke heart with little resistance. Broil the artichokes, cut-side up, for 8 to 10 minutes until the artichokes are well charred.

SUGAR SNAP PEAS WITH HORSERADISH GREMOLATA AND RADISHES

This fresh, springlike side dish gets a double dose of spicy from the horse-radish and the radishes. It's great served alongside rich main dishes like grilled lamb chops or on top of a bed of warm, creamy white beans, for a complete veg meal.

¼ cup [10 g] Grilled Bread Crumbs (see page 38)
2 Tbsp finely grated fresh horseradish
2 Tbsp finely chopped flat-leaf parsley
1 tsp lemon zest
2 Tbsp extra-virgin olive oil
1 lb [455 g] sugar snap peas
Kosher salt
4 radishes, thinly sliced

In a small bowl, stir together the bread crumbs, horseradish, parsley, and lemon zest. Drizzle 1 Tbsp of the oil over the mixture and stir so everything is a bit moist. Set the gremolata aside.

Toss the sugar snap peas with another 1 Tbsp of oil and sprinkle with salt. Heat the grill to medium-high and, using a grill topper, cook the sugar snap peas until they are crisp-tender and charred in spots, 3 to 4 minutes. Transfer to a bowl and top with the sliced radishes and gremolata. Serve immediately.

INDOOR METHOD: Prepare the gremolata as directed. Then heat a medium cast-iron or other skillet over high heat and ready the sugar snap peas for cooking. When the skillet is very hot, add the sugar snaps and cook, tossing, until the pods are charred in spots and cooked through. Proceed as directed above.

CHARRED GREEN BEANS WITH TAHINI

This green bean dish takes its cues from a similar one served at Zahav, in Philadelphia. Like the restaurant's, this one has all of the creaminess of the classic casserole, complete with an oniony lid and some toasty almonds. It happens to be vegan, it can be gluten-free (just leave the flour off the shallots), and it certainly wouldn't feel out of place on a Thanksgiving table.

¼ cup [45 g] uncooked quinoa, rinsed
1 tsp kosher salt, plus more as needed
5 Tbsp [120 ml] vegetable oil
¼ cup [30 g] almonds, coarsely chopped
Fried Shallots (page 33)
½ cup [110 g] tahini
1 tsp lemon zest, plus juice from 1 lemon
1 small garlic clove, grated
2 Tbsp packed finely chopped flat-leaf parsley
1 lb [455 g] green beans, ends trimmed
Cilantro, for garnish
Flaky salt, such as Maldon, for finishing

To make the quinoa: Bring the quinoa, ⅓ cup [80 ml] water, and ½ tsp salt to a boil in a small saucepan. Reduce the heat and simmer until the water is absorbed and the quinoa still has some bite, about 10 minutes. Quinoa can be cooked in advance. If you're not frying it right away, spread it out on a plate so it can dry out.

In a medium skillet, heat 3 Tbsp of the oil. When the oil shimmers, add the cooked quinoa and fry, stirring often, until the grains are evenly browned and crispy, about 7 minutes. In the last minute or two of cooking, add the almonds to the skillet and continue to stir. Transfer the quinoa and almonds to a bowl and wipe out the skillet to prepare the shallots. Set both aside.

To make the dressing: Stir together the tahini with the lemon zest, juice, garlic, ½ tsp salt, parsley, and ¼ cup [60 ml] water. Add more water, a tablespoon at a time, until the dressing is creamy and pourable. Taste often and adjust until the sauce is balanced among tahini, lemon, and salt.

Heat your grill to medium-high. Toss the green beans with the remaining 2 Tbsp oil and sprinkle with salt. Grill on a grill topper, tossing occasionally, until the beans are crisp-tender and have char marks, 6 to 7 minutes. Transfer the green beans to a large shallow bowl and toss with the dressing until they are very well coated. Top the beans with the crispy quinoa and almonds and then the shallots. Garnish with cilantro and a sprinkling of flaky salt. The crispy quinoa with almonds, fried shallots, and tahini dressing can all be made earlier in the day. Keep all of the components at room temperature and assemble just before serving.

INDOOR METHOD: Prepare the quinoa and dressing as directed. Preheat the broiler and prepare the green beans for cooking as directed. Then, on a foil-lined baking sheet, broil the green beans until charred and blistered in spots and cooked through, 7 to 8 minutes. Continue as directed.

CHARRED EDAMAME WITH SESAME, GINGER, AND SOY

This popular sushi bar snack gets a lift from some smoky char, salty soy, and a hit of fresh ginger.

2 Tbsp soy sauce

2 tsp toasted sesame oil

1 tsp fresh ginger, finely grated

1 lb [455 g] fresh or frozen edamame in their pods, rinsed

Togarashi or toasted sesame seeds, for finishing (optional)

In a small bowl, combine the soy sauce, sesame oil, and ginger. Set the sauce aside.

Heat the grill to medium and top with a mesh grill topper. Shake any excess water off the edamame and grill until they are charred in spots and heated through, about 5 minutes. Transfer to a bowl and toss with the sauce until each pod is well coated. Finish with togarashi if desired. Serve immediately.

INDOOR METHOD: Prepare the sauce and ready the edamame for cooking as directed. Then heat a medium cast-iron or other skillet over high heat. When the skillet is very hot, add the edamame and cook, tossing, until the pods are charred in spots and heated through. Proceed as directed above.

CHARRED LEEKS WITH BLUE CHEESE AND WALNUTS

This dish is about as far from a wan slice of grilled zucchini as you can get. Leeks get sweet and supple on the grill, with some crisp, charred edges, and then are dressed up with refined Waldorf flavors. If spring onions are in season near you, they would be delicious here as well.

2 Tbsp red wine vinegar

1 tsp coarse-grained Dijon mustard

¼ tsp kosher salt, plus more as needed

Freshly ground black pepper

1 tsp finely chopped fresh tarragon leaves

2 Tbsp extra-virgin olive oil, plus more for brushing

2 small leeks, white and pale green parts only

3 oz [85 g] blue cheese

¼ cup [30 g] walnuts, toasted and coarsely chopped

½ crisp apple, such as Gala, thinly sliced

To make the vinaigrette: In a small bowl or jar, combine the vinegar, mustard, ¼ tsp of the salt, pepper, tarragon, and 2 Tbsp of oil and mix or shake well.

To prepare the leeks: Heat your grill to high. Trim off the dark green parts, cut them in half lengthwise, and rinse well, gently separating the layers under running water to remove all of the sand. Brush both sides with olive oil and sprinkle with salt. Grill, flipping once, until both sides are charred and the leeks are softened but not at all mushy, 3 to 4 minutes per side.

When the leeks are cooked, transfer to a platter or divide among four plates. Drizzle with the vinaigrette and crumble the blue cheese over. Top with walnuts and apple slices. Serve immediately. Note: the leeks can be grilled an hour or two ahead of time and served at room temperature. Just assemble the salad right before serving.

INDOOR METHOD: Prepare the vinaigrette and the leeks as directed. Then heat a large cast-iron skillet over medium-high heat. Add the leeks to the grill pan, cut-side down. Cook until deeply brown on the cut side, about 6 minutes. Flip and cook for another few minutes until tender all the way through, but not overly soft. Continue as directed.

MUSHROOM-FARRO VEGGIE BURGERS

This seems like a lot of steps and parts, but hang in there; this is the best veggie burger you'll ever have. Each ingredient adds either great flavor or crucial texture. (No one likes mushy veggie burgers.) Moisture makes veggie burgers stick, so be sure to roast your chickpeas long enough, drain any excess liquid from the farro, and wring out those porcinis before you throw them into the food processor. And just to be on the safe side, oil the burgers and the grill.

½ cup [90 g] uncooked farro

One 15.5-oz [440-g] can chickpeas

½ oz [15 g] dried porcini mushrooms

4 Tbsp [60 ml] extra-virgin olive oil

3 oz [80 g] cremini or other fresh mushrooms, thinly sliced

1 shallot, finely chopped

Kosher salt

1 medium carrot, coarsely chopped

1 Tbsp miso paste

1 Tbsp soy sauce

Freshly ground black pepper

1 egg, lightly beaten

4 slices of cheese (optional)

4 hamburger buns

Topping suggestions (all optional): grilled avocado, lettuce, tomato, Fire-Roasted Ketchup (page 23), Classic Aioli (page 20)

In a small pot, cook the farro with ⅔ the amount of water directed on the package, until it's just cooked through and still quite chewy. Drain any excess cooking liquid.

Preheat the oven to 400°F [200°C]. Line a small baking sheet with aluminum foil. Drain and rinse the chickpeas. Lay half on your prepared baking sheet and roast in the oven until golden and crisp, about 20 minutes. Reserve the other half.

In a small bowl or measuring cup, cover the porcinis with very hot water and let stand 20 minutes.

In a medium skillet, heat 2 Tbsp of oil over medium-high heat. Add the shallot and sauté until slightly softened and beginning to turn golden, about 3 minutes. Add the cremini and porcini mushrooms (drain the soaking liquid) and a big pinch of salt and stir occasionally until they are deeply browned and cooked through, 8 to 10 minutes. Transfer to the bowl of a food processor and wipe out the skillet.

Add the cooked and drained farro, all of the chickpeas (roasted and unroasted), the carrot, the miso paste, and the soy sauce to the processor. Pulse several times until the mixture is fairly uniform but still has lots of texture. Transfer the burger mixture to a large bowl, season with salt and pepper, and add the egg. Mix until thoroughly combined.

Line a plate with parchment or wax paper and shape the burger mixture into 4 patties. Chill in the refrigerator, uncovered, for at least an hour or overnight, flipping once, so both sides dry out slightly. The uncooked patties keep for up to 3 days, refrigerated, wrapped in plastic wrap.

To cook, heat the grill to medium-high and clean and oil the grate. Brush both sides of each burger with the remaining olive oil and sprinkle with salt and pepper. Grill the burgers until they are deeply browned, about 4 minutes per side, adding cheese, if using, during the last minute on the second side. Serve immediately on hamburger buns with your favorite burger toppings.

INDOOR METHOD: Prepare the burger mixture and form patties as directed. Heat a cast-iron or other skillet over medium heat. Add 3 Tbsp olive or vegetable oil to the skillet, and when the oil starts to shimmer, add the burgers, taking care not to crowd them. Fry them until crisp and golden on both sides and cooked through, about 7 minutes per side.

FALAFEL-STYLE VEGGIE BURGERS

Here's the PSA—the public-service announcement—of the book: falafel is not hard to make, especially if you skip the part where you fry the patties. (Thank you, grill!) The trickiest part is remembering to soak the chickpeas the night before and also to oil, oil, oil, oil everything. This falafel is especially delicious doused in Green Goddess Dressing (page 16).

1 cup [180 g] dried chickpeas

1 Tbsp extra-virgin olive oil,
   plus more for brushing the patties

½ yellow onion, finely chopped

1 large garlic clove, minced

½ cup [20 g] coarsely chopped flat-leaf parsley

½ cup [20 g] coarsely chopped cilantro

¼ tsp cayenne pepper

½ tsp ground cumin

½ tsp ground coriander

2 Tbsp toasted sesame seeds

½ tsp baking powder

1½ tsp kosher salt, plus more as needed

3 to 4 Tbsp all-purpose flour

2 eggs, lightly beaten

Hamburger buns or pitas, Green Goddess
   Dressing (page 16), or Charred Beet Hummus
   (page 24), cucumber slices, and chopped
   tomato for serving (optional)

In a large bowl or container, cover the chickpeas by at least 2 to 3 inches [5 to 7.5 cm] with cold water. Refrigerate for at least 8 hours or overnight.

Heat 1 Tbsp of the oil in a medium skillet over high heat. When the oil is shimmering, add the onion and cook for 2 minutes. Add the garlic and sauté the mixture until the onion is browned at the edges and translucent in the middle, about 2 minutes more. Let the onion and garlic cool slightly and then transfer to the bowl of a food processor.

Drain the chickpeas, transfer them to the food processor with the onion and garlic, and add the parsley, cilantro, cayenne, cumin, and coriander. Pulse several times until the mixture is evenly minced but not yet pasty.

Transfer the mixture to a large bowl. Sprinkle in the sesame seeds, baking powder, 1½ tsp of salt, and 3 Tbsp of the flour and then add the eggs. Mix until thoroughly combined. If the mixture looks too wet, add the additional 1 Tbsp flour. Line a plate with parchment or wax paper, form the mixture into 4 patties, and put them on the plate. Chill the patties, uncovered, in the refrigerator for at least an hour and up to 4 hours. The falafel mixture can be made up to 2 days in advance; store in an airtight container, refrigerated. Before using, form into patties and allow to dry out as directed above.

Heat your grill to medium and clean and oil the grate. Brush one side of the patties liberally with additional oil and season with salt. Using a light hand, gently put the falafel patties on the grill, oiled sides down, and cook, undisturbed, until the bottoms are golden and have nice char marks, about 8 minutes. Then brush the top side of each patty with oil and sprinkle with salt. Gently flip the patties and cook until both sides are golden and charred, another 4 to 5 minutes.

Serve with hamburger buns or pitas, dressing or hummus, and sliced cucumbers and tomatoes, if desired.

INDOOR METHOD: Prepare the falafel mixture and patties as directed. Heat a cast-iron or other skillet over medium heat. Add 3 Tbsp olive oil to the skillet and, when the oil starts to shimmer, add the patties, taking care not to crowd them. Fry the patties until crisp and golden on both sides and cooked through, 5 to 7 minutes per side. Serve as directed.

QUINOA TABBOULEH STUFFED PEPPERS

Skip those grilled veggie kebabs. This is an elegant presentation for a substantial, yet refreshing, vegetarian meal. Want to make it more substantial (and less vegetarian)? Sauté some minced onion with ground lamb and add that to the peppers before stuffing them with tabbouleh.

1 cup [180 g] uncooked quinoa

1 English cucumber, diced

1 cup [150 g] cherry tomatoes, halved

½ cup [80 g] salt-cured olives, pitted and chopped

3 green onions, finely chopped

2 cups [35 g] finely chopped flat-leaf parsley

½ cup [20 g] finely chopped fresh mint leaves

¼ cup [60 ml] plus 2 Tbsp extra-virgin olive oil

Juice from 1½ lemons (approximately 4 to 5 Tbsp/60 to 75 ml)

Kosher salt

Freshly ground black pepper

4 red bell peppers

4 oz [110 g] feta cheese, cut into 8 slices, plus more for topping (optional)

In a medium saucepan, bring the quinoa and 2 cups [480 ml] of water to a boil, reduce heat to medium-low, and simmer until the quinoa is cooked through and all of the water is absorbed, 10 to 15 minutes.

Meanwhile, in a large bowl, combine the cucumber, tomatoes, olives, green onions, parsley, and mint. In a measuring cup or small bowl, combine the ¼ cup [60 ml] olive oil and the lemon juice. Season with salt and freshly ground pepper. When the quinoa is done, add it to the bowl with the vegetables and herbs. Pour the dressing over all and toss well until the ingredients are fully combined. Taste and adjust the seasoning of the tabbouleh before setting aside.

Preheat your grill to medium. Cut the bell peppers in half lengthwise and remove the seeds and ribs. Brush the peppers with the remaining 2 Tbsp of olive oil and sprinkle the inside with a pinch of salt. Grill the peppers, cut-side down, until they take on grill marks and begin to soften, 2 to 3 minutes. Flip and place a slice of feta cheese in the cavity of each pepper. Grill until the outsides of the peppers have grill marks and the cheese is slightly melted, another 5 to 6 minutes.

Remove the peppers from the grill and fill each pepper cavity with tabbouleh, topping with more feta, if desired. Serve hot or at room temperature.

INDOOR METHOD: Preheat the oven to 400°F [200°C]. Prepare the tabbouleh and peppers as directed. On a foil-lined baking sheet, roast the peppers, cut-side down, until they start to soften, 10 to 12 minutes. Flip the peppers, fill with feta, and roast until the cheese is melted and the peppers are cooked through, about 8 minutes more. Proceed as directed.

CORN, MUSHROOMS, ROOTS, AND BREAD

MEXICAN STREET CORN

Corn on the cob is undoubtedly one of the best things about summer. This version gets a bit of a char from the grill, some tangy creaminess from the yogurt mixture, and that satisfying salty bite from the cheese. If you can't find cotija, substitute Parmesan, finely grated either by hand or in a food processor.

2 Tbsp plain, full-fat Greek yogurt

2 Tbsp mayonnaise or Classic Aioli and Variations (page 20)

1 Tbsp finely chopped fresh cilantro

1 tsp fresh lime juice

6 oz [170 g] very finely crumbled cotija cheese

¼ tsp chili powder

4 ears of corn, shucked

In a small bowl, stir together the yogurt, mayonnaise, cilantro, and lime juice. In another small bowl, finely crumble the cheese by hand or pulse it in a food processor. (The finer it is, the more easily it will stick to the corn.) Mix the chili powder into the cheese and spread out the mixture on a plate.

Heat your grill to medium, and grill the corn until well charred on all sides, 10 to 15 minutes total. While the corn is hot, slather with a thin layer of the yogurt-mayo mixture and roll in the cheese until the corn is covered in a light, even layer. The corn, yogurt-mayonnaise mixture, and cheese can all be prepared several hours in advance. Assemble just before serving.

INDOOR METHOD: Prepare the yogurt-mayo mixture and cheese as directed. Preparing to cook the corn, line your stovetop with foil to make for easier cleanup. Turn a burner to medium-high and, using tongs, cook the corn directly over the flame, turning often, until well charred on all sides. Proceed as directed.

CORN SALAD WITH MISO AND FRESH AND GRILLED CUCUMBERS

This recipe is a summer grilling staple and is endlessly adaptable. Use whatever veggies you have around (crunchy ones like snap peas and radishes are nice for contrast), and any kind of miso. Just don't skip it or the herbs.

2 Tbsp butter, at room temperature
2 Tbsp miso paste
4 ears of corn, shucked
2 Tbsp vegetable oil
Kosher salt
1 English cucumber
1 cup [160 g] cherry tomatoes, halved
1 cup [115 g] sugar snap peas, thinly sliced
6 radishes, thinly sliced
1 cup [about 40 g] finely chopped fresh herbs, such as parsley, cilantro, or mint, or a combination
Freshly ground black pepper

Mix together the butter and the miso paste until combined. Set aside.

Heat the grill to medium-high. Brush the corn with some of the oil and sprinkle with salt. Cut the cucumber in half across the middle, so you have two long pieces. Slice both halves again in half lengthwise. Reserve two of the pieces to use raw; brush the cut sides of the other two pieces with oil and season with salt. Grill the corn, turning occasionally, until all sides are evenly charred in spots and the kernels are cooked through, 10 to 15 minutes. At the same time, grill the cucumber pieces, cut-side down, until you see nice char marks. Transfer the corn and cucumber to a baking sheet, and, while the corn is hot, carefully cut the kernels off the cobs and put them in a large bowl. Add the miso butter and toss to coat.

Cut both the grilled and fresh cucumber into ¼-in [6-mm] half-moon-shaped slices and add those to the bowl as well. Add the tomatoes, sugar snap peas, radishes, and herbs and toss to combine. Sprinkle with salt and pepper and toss. Adjust the seasoning. This salad can be made up to 4 hours in advance. Keep at room temperature and add the herbs just before serving.

INDOOR METHOD: Prepare the miso butter, the corn, and the cucumber as directed. Heat a cast-iron or other skillet large enough to hold all of the corn kernels over medium-high heat. Add 1 Tbsp oil. Once the oil is shimmering, add two pieces of the cucumber, cut-side down, until they are seared and brown, about 2 minutes. Remove the cucumber and set aside. Reserve the skillet.

Carefully cut the corn kernels off the cobs. Heat the same skillet over medium-high heat. Cook the corn, tossing often, until the kernels are brown in spots and cooked through. Add the miso butter to the skillet and stir until the butter is melted and all of the kernels are glossy and coated. Transfer the corn to a bowl and proceed as directed.

MUSHROOM AND TOFU SPRING ROLLS

It takes some practice to get the hang of rolling these spring rolls, but even if they look a little wonky at first, they'll taste delicious. Also, it looks like a lot of parts and pieces, but they come together pretty easily. If you're not into the Peanut Dipping Sauce that accompanies this recipe, try the Fish Sauce Vinaigrette (page 79) or the Carrot Ginger Dressing (page 129) instead.

7 oz [200 g] extra-firm tofu

Teriyaki Sauce (page 29) or store-bought

6 oz [200 g] assorted mushrooms (shiitakes work well here)

3 Tbsp vegetable oil, plus more for brushing

Kosher salt

2 small Persian or Japanese cucumbers, or ½ English cucumber

1 head of Little Gem lettuce or romaine

Rice paper wrappers

Pickled Carrots (page 30)

20 fresh mint leaves

¼ cup [10 g] chopped fresh cilantro

Peanut Dipping Sauce (recipe follows)

On a plate, cutting board, or baking sheet, wrap the tofu in several layers of paper towels. Place another plate or baking sheet on top and weigh down with books, cans, or other heavy items to remove as much moisture as possible. Let the tofu sit for at least half an hour and up to 6 hours—the longer the better.

Unwrap the tofu. Cut the block into ½-in [12-mm] planks and lay out on a plate or cutting board. Brush with enough teriyaki sauce to coat and let stand until the sauce soaks in, about 30 minutes.

Gently clean the mushrooms with a damp paper towel and then cut them in halves or quarters so they are bite-size. In a medium bowl, toss the mushrooms with 1½ Tbsp of the oil and some salt.

Heat your grill to medium-high. Grill the mushrooms using a grill topper, tossing occasionally, until they are charred and crispy in spots, 8 to 10 minutes. Brush both sides of the tofu with oil and grill until the slices have even grill marks on both sides and are heated through, 3 to 4 minutes per side. When the mushrooms are done, transfer to a bowl. When the tofu is done, transfer to a plate.

Cut the tofu planks into strips ½ in [12 mm] wide and set aside. Cut the cucumber into thin matchsticks and separate the leaves of the lettuce.

To assemble the spring rolls, prepare plenty of workspace. Here's the setup: rice paper wrappers to one side, a pie plate or large bowl with hot tap water (for dipping the wrappers in) next to it, a clean space (cutting board or plate) for wrapping, then all of your other spring roll components, and a plate or platter on which to place the finished rolls.

To roll, submerge a wrapper completely in the water and lay it out on the cutting board. It should be wet, but only wet enough so that it's pliable without cracking. It will continue to soften as you're working. Lay down a lettuce leaf first (this helps keep all of the ingredients in place), with the top edge toward the top right part of the wrapper (about two o'clock). Then add a strip of tofu on top of the lettuce leaf, 2 Tbsp or so of mushrooms, 2 or 3 pieces of cucumber and carrot, 2 or 3 mint leaves, and a sprinkling of cilantro. Starting with the right edge of the wrapper, fold it in over the fillings, trying to keep everything tight and in place. Fold up the bottom edge, and continue to roll from right to left until you have a compact roll that's closed at the bottom and open at the top.

Repeat with the remaining ingredients and serve with the peanut dipping sauce on the side. Spring rolls can be made up to 3 hours in advance. If not serving immediately, keep them at room temperature, tightly covered with plastic wrap so that they do not dry out.

INDOOR METHOD: Prepare the tofu and mushrooms for cooking. Heat a cast-iron or other skillet over medium heat. Add 2 Tbsp vegetable oil to the skillet, and when the oil is shimmering, add the tofu slices, taking care not to crowd them. Fry them until crisp and golden on both sides and warmed all the way through. When the tofu is done, transfer to a plate. Wipe out the skillet and add an additional 2 Tbsp vegetable oil. Add the mushrooms and cook, stirring occasionally, until they are golden brown in spots and cooked through. Transfer the mushrooms to a plate and proceed as directed.

PEANUT DIPPING SAUCE

This peanut sauce is also slightly adapted from the blog *Dinner: A Love Story*. As writer Jenny Rosenstrach notes, it's delicious stirred into noodles as well as puddled on top of sautéed spinach. Any kind of peanut butter works, since the blender smooths out everything.

One 1-in [2.5-cm] piece fresh ginger, peeled
1 garlic clove, peeled
½ cup [130 g] peanut butter
2 Tbsp soy sauce
1 Tbsp rice wine vinegar
1 Tbsp toasted sesame oil
1 tsp agave syrup or honey

Combine the ginger, garlic, peanut butter, soy sauce, vinegar, oil, agave syrup, and ½ cup [120 ml] water in a blender or food processor and blend until smooth. This can be made up to 3 days ahead. Store in an airtight container, refrigerated.

MIXED GRILL MUSHROOMS OVER POLENTA

This is a rich, comforting dish that comes together fast. While gremolata is traditionally used with savory braised meats, this almond version lends crunch and some extra oomph here. Any leftover polenta can be poured into a baking dish, chilled, cut into squares or triangles, oiled, and grilled for a different take on the same dish.

⅓ cup [40 g] almonds, well toasted and coarsely chopped

¼ cup [10 g] finely chopped flat-leaf parsley

Zest from 1 lemon

3 to 4 cups [720 to 960 ml] water

1 cup [140 g] uncooked polenta

2 tsp kosher salt, plus more for tossing

½ cup [15 g] finely grated Parmesan cheese

3 Tbsp butter, or 2 Tbsp mascarpone cheese or crème fraîche and 1 Tbsp butter

1 lb [455 g] assorted mushrooms

2 to 3 Tbsp extra-virgin olive oil

½ tsp finely chopped fresh thyme leaves

To make the gremolata, in a small bowl, combine the almonds, parsley, and lemon zest. Set aside.

In a medium saucepan, combine the water (using the amount specified on the package), polenta, and 2 tsp salt and bring to a boil over high heat. Lower heat to a simmer, cover, and cook, stirring occasionally, until the polenta is smooth and creamy, 10 to 15 minutes. Turn off the heat and whisk in the Parmesan cheese and

Gently clean the mushrooms with a damp paper towel and trim the ends. Cut larger mushrooms into bite-size pieces. In a medium bowl, toss the mushrooms with 2 to 3 Tbsp of olive oil and salt. Heat your grill to high and, using a grill topper, cook the mushrooms until they're crisp and golden, 10 to 12 minutes. Transfer the mushrooms back to the bowl that you used before and toss with the remaining 1 Tbsp of butter and the thyme.

If you need to reheat the polenta, stir over medium heat, adding water a few tablespoons at a time, until it is hot and creamy again. Divide the polenta among four shallow bowls. Top the polenta with mushrooms and sprinkle generously with the gremolata. Serve immediately.

INDOOR METHOD: Prepare the gremolata and polenta and clean and cut the mushrooms as directed. Heat a medium cast-iron or other skillet over medium-high heat. Skip oiling the mushrooms ahead of time and instead add 2 Tbsp olive oil and 1 Tbsp butter to the skillet. When the oil is shimmering and the butter is melted, add the mushrooms, taking care not to crowd them (divide into two batches, if necessary). Let the mushrooms cook for several minutes without stirring or flipping, until the underside is golden and crisp. Flip or stir the mushrooms and cook until both sides are well browned, about 10 minutes total. Stir in the thyme leaves and season with salt. Proceed with the remainder of the recipe as directed.

TERIYAKI MUSHROOM BOWLS WITH TOGARASHI

The teriyaki sauce used here is simple (five ingredients!), versatile, and has many fewer things in it (in a good way) than whatever you would buy in a bottle. (But don't worry; store-bought teriyaki sauce totally works here, too.) The rice bowls themselves are endlessly adaptable. You can add grilled tofu, any number of vegetables—whether raw, grilled, or pickled (carrots, cucumber, snap peas, edamame, sautéed spinach). Below is the very simplest way to go.

1 cup [200 g] uncooked white or brown rice

1 lb [455 g] assorted mushrooms

3 Tbsp vegetable oil

Kosher salt

Teriyaki Sauce (page 29)

2 celery stalks, very thinly sliced on the diagonal

1 avocado, peeled and quartered

¼ cup [10 g] chopped fresh cilantro, for garnish

Togarashi, for garnish

Cook the rice as directed on the package.

Gently clean the mushrooms with a damp paper towel. In a medium bowl, toss the mushrooms with the oil and 1 tsp salt until well coated. Heat your grill to medium-high and, using a grill topper, cook the mushrooms until well charred and crispy on the edges, about 10 minutes total. When the mushrooms are finished, return them to the bowl you used before and toss with ½ of the teriyaki sauce to coat while they're hot.

To assemble the bowls, divide the rice among four bowls and top with the mushrooms, celery, and avocado. Garnish with cilantro and togarashi. Serve with the remaining sauce on the side.

INDOOR METHOD: Prepare the rice and clean the mushrooms as directed. Heat a medium cast-iron or other skillet over medium-high heat. Skip oiling the mushrooms ahead of time and instead add 2 Tbsp vegetable oil to the skillet. When the oil is shimmering, add the mushrooms, taking care not to crowd them (divide into two batches, if necessary). Let the mushrooms cook for several minutes without stirring or flipping, until the undersides are golden and crisp. Flip or stir the mushrooms, and cook until both sides are well browned, about 10 minutes total. Transfer the mushrooms to a bowl and toss with enough teriyaki sauce to coat. Assemble the bowls as directed.

CARROTS WITH MISO BUTTER, CHICKPEAS, AND CILANTRO

In this lush carrot dish, mixing the hot, freshly grilled carrots with the miso butter ensures that every bite is glazed with that rich miso flavor. The chickpeas make this a substantial meal, and the seaweed (like the kind that comes in snack packs) adds a wonderful salinity.

1 lb [455 g] carrots

3 Tbsp extra-virgin olive oil

1 tsp toasted sesame oil

Kosher salt

4 Tbsp butter, at room temperature

2 Tbsp miso paste

1 Tbsp mirin

One 15.5-oz [445-g] can chickpeas, drained and rinsed

¼ cup [15 g] cilantro, chopped

Toasted nori seaweed, for garnish

Peel the carrots. If your carrots are small, use as is; if they're larger, cut in half once crosswise and once lengthwise until you have sticks that are about ¾ in [2 cm] by 4 or 5 in [10 to 12 cm]. Toss with the olive and sesame oils and sprinkle with salt. Grill the carrots over medium-high heat, turning occasionally, until they are evenly charred and tender but not mushy, about 10 minutes.

While the carrots are grilling, stir together the softened butter, miso, and mirin. When the carrots are cooked, transfer to a bowl, and while they're very hot, toss with the miso butter and chickpeas. Sprinkle with cilantro and crumble toasted seaweed over the top. Serve immediately.

INDOOR METHOD: Preheat the broiler. Trim, oil, and season the carrots as directed. On a foil-lined baking sheet, broil the carrots, tossing once halfway through, until they are well charred in spots and tender, 8 to 10 minutes. Proceed with the remainder of the recipe as directed.

CARROTS WITH GRILLED CITRUS, AVOCADO, PISTACHIOS, AND ALL OF THE SEEDS

This dish is inspired by a roasted carrot salad at ABC Kitchen in New York. It has a bit of everything: earthiness from the carrots and pimentón, cool creaminess from the avocado, a satisfying nutty crunch from the seeds, and a lovely sweetness from the grilled citrus dressing. If you don't feel like getting all of the seeds, just bump up the amount of the ones you are using.

1 Tbsp sesame seeds
1 Tbsp roasted unsalted sunflower seeds
2 Tbsp roasted unsalted pumpkin seeds
¼ cup [80 g] roasted unsalted shelled pistachios
Kosher salt
1 lb [455 g] carrots
⅓ cup [80 ml] plus 3 Tbsp extra-virgin olive oil
2 tsp pimentón or smoked paprika
1 navel orange
1 lemon
2 Tbsp apple cider vinegar
Freshly ground black pepper
2 cups [40 g] arugula
2 avocados, peeled and cut into 8 wedges each

In a clean, dry skillet over medium heat, toast all seeds and nuts one kind at a time. Beginning with the sesame seeds, add the seeds to the skillet and stir often until they begin to smell nutty and turn golden, about 2 minutes. (Watch carefully; they go from golden to burnt in a blink). Transfer the seeds to a medium bowl, and repeat the process with the sunflower seeds. Follow with the pumpkin seeds, toasting for 3 or 4 minutes, and adding each to the bowl with the sesame seeds. Finally, toast the pistachios. When they begin to smell fragrant and turn brown in spots, about 6 minutes, move them to a cutting board and coarsely chop them, or place them in a zip-top bag and crush them lightly. Add them to the bowl with all of the other seeds and a big pinch of salt. Set aside.

Peel the carrots. If your carrots are small, leave them whole. If they're larger than ¾ in [2 cm] or so in diameter, cut them in half once crosswise and once lengthwise to make carrot sticks. Toss with 3 Tbsp of the olive oil and sprinkle generously with kosher salt and the pimentón. Heat your grill to medium and cook until there are even grill marks and the carrots are softened but not at all mushy, 4 to 5 minutes per side. When the carrots are done, transfer them to a platter.

CONTINUED

While you're grilling the carrots, cut the orange and lemon in half and add both to the grill, cut-side down. Cook until the fruit has softened and caramelized, about 6 minutes.

When the citrus is done, remove from the grill. When cool enough to handle, squeeze the orange and lemon halves into a measuring cup until you have ½ cup [120 ml] of juice. Whisk in the apple cider vinegar, ½ tsp of salt, freshly ground pepper, and the remaining ⅓ cup [80 ml] of olive oil.

To assemble, toss the arugula with a few table-spoons of the dressing and lay on a platter. Add the carrots, arrange the avocado slices around and over the carrots, and drizzle with more dressing. (You may not use it all.) Top with the seeds and serve.

The dressing keeps refrigerated for 1 week. Store any extra seed mix in an airtight container at room temperature for up to 1 month.

INDOOR METHOD: Prepare the seeds and nuts as directed. Preheat the broiler. Trim, oil, and season the carrots as directed; cut the citrus, too. Place the carrots and citrus on a foil-lined baking sheet. Broil, tossing once halfway through, until they are well charred in spots and tender, 8 to 10 minutes. Proceed with the remainder of the recipe as directed.

SMOKED BEETS WITH DILL YOGURT DRESSING AND RYE BREAD CRUMBS

This technique for smoking the beets couldn't be easier. The flavors of the yogurt, dill, green onion, and rye add a little bit of a delicious "everything bagel with cream cheese" flavor.

8 small beets with their greens

4 Tbsp [120 ml] extra-virgin olive oil

Kosher salt

2 green onions

1 English cucumber

1 cup [240 g] plain Greek yogurt

1 Tbsp finely chopped dill

2 tsp sherry vinegar

2 slices [120 g] dark rye bread (or enough to make about 1½ cups torn crumbs)

2 Tbsp butter

2 cups [40 g] arugula or baby kale

Flaky salt, such as Maldon, for finishing

To prepare the beets, cut off the greens and wash both bulbs and greens thoroughly, leaving water clinging to the leaves. Fold two very large pieces of heavy-duty aluminum foil in half, so the space you have to work with is roughly 12 by 24 in [30 by 60 cm] each. Divide the beet greens in half and lay one half on each piece of foil. Divide the beets and lay them on top of each beet green bed. Drizzle the beets with 2 Tbsp of the oil and sprinkle generously with salt. Fold up the foil to create two pack-ets, tightly crimping the edges. With a knife, poke several holes in the foil to allow the smoke from the coals to permeate and cook the beets.

Heat a charcoal grill to medium and place each packet directly in the coals of the grill, carefully using a grill shovel to put some of the coals on top of the packets as well. If using a gas grill, the beets will still cook, but they'll have a more subtle smoky flavor. Roast the beets for 30 to 40 minutes (start with the greens beneath the beets), flipping the packets halfway through the grilling time. The beets are done when a knife easily slips through them. (You can test doneness right through the foil.)

CONTINUED

While the beets are roasting, grill the green onions on the grill grate until softened and charred in spots. When the green onions are cool enough to handle, finely slice them (a pair of scissors works well here) and set aside.

Finely chop ⅓ of the cucumber. Thinly slice the remaining ⅔ and set this portion aside. Mix together the yogurt, green onions, dill, finely chopped cucumber, vinegar, and a big pinch of salt in a small bowl. Set aside.

To prepare the bread crumbs, tear the bread slices into roughly pea-size pieces. In a medium skillet over medium-high heat, heat the remaining 2 Tbsp oil and the butter. Line a plate with paper towels. When the butter is melted and foamy, add the bread crumbs, season with salt, and fry, stirring often, until the bread crumbs are toasted and crispy. Transfer the crumbs to the paper towel–lined plate.

Once the beets are cooked through, remove the packets from the grill. A baking sheet is a good landing spot. Carefully open the foil and remove the beets. Discard the foil and charred greens. When the beets are cool enough to handle, slip off the skins and cut into quarters. (Wear gloves if you don't want pink fingers while doing this.). Divide the arugula and sliced cucumbers among four plates. Arrange the beets on top, spoon the yogurt mixture over all, shower with crispy bread crumbs, and finish with flaky salt.

The beets, yogurt mixture, and bread crumbs can all be made up to 1 day in advance. Keep the beets and yogurt refrigerated and store the bread crumbs in an airtight container at room temperature. Bring the beets to room temperature before using. Assemble just before serving.

INDOOR METHOD: Preheat the oven to 375°F [190°C]. Wash and trim the beets, discarding the beet greens or reserving them for another use. Wrap each beet individually in foil, and place all of the beets on a baking sheet. Roast in the oven until the beets are tender and can be easily pierced with a sharp knife, 45 to 60 minutes. Proceed with the remainder of the recipe as directed.

FENNEL WITH HERBED RICOTTA

This dish has a lovely, subtle anise flavor from the fennel and a creamy luxuriousness from the ricotta. Serve with crackers for an elegant summer starter.

1 cup [250 g] ricotta cheese

¼ cup [8 g] finely grated Parmesan or pecorino romano cheese

Leaves from 1 sprig thyme, finely chopped

3 Tbsp finely chopped flat-leaf parsley

2 Tbsp finely chopped fresh mint

1 Tbsp finely chopped fresh chives

Kosher salt

Freshly ground black pepper

1 lemon

3 fennel bulbs, fronds reserved for garnish

2 Tbsp extra-virgin olive oil

In a medium bowl, mix the ricotta and Parmesan cheeses, herbs, a big pinch of salt, and several grinds of pepper. Zest the whole lemon, cut it in half, and juice one half. Add the zest and juice to the mixture and reserve the other lemon half. Set the ricotta mixture aside (for as long as several hours, refrigerated) for its flavors to develop.

Pick off some of the more delicate fennel fronds and set aside for the garnish. Slice each fennel bulb in half lengthwise and remove the outermost layer, which can be kind of tough. Cut each half into 4 wedges, keeping the root end of each wedge as intact as possible. In a bowl, toss with the oil and sprinkle with salt.

Heat your grill to medium-high and cook the fennel until the underside has grill marks and has started to caramelize, about 6 minutes. Flip each wedge over and grill another 5 to 6 minutes, until the vegetables are softened but still hold their shape and the edges are a bit charred.

Remove the fennel from the grill, squeeze the juice from the remaining lemon half over the vegetables, and transfer to four individual plates or a platter. Dollop the herbed ricotta alongside the fennel or serve it in a bowl on the side. Garnish with the reserved fennel fronds or additional chopped herbs.

INDOOR METHOD: Prepare the ricotta mixture as directed. Preheat the oven to 375°F [190°C]. Trim, oil, and season the fennel as directed. On a baking sheet, roast the fennel, flipping once halfway through, until it's nicely caramelized and cooked through, about 20 minutes total. Proceed with the remainder of the recipe as directed.

BABY TURNIPS AND GREENS WITH CARROT GINGER DRESSING

This dish feels decadent and buttery, without having any butter in it at all. The turnips get sweet, the greens feel wholesome, and the carrot ginger dressing is just a little bit luxurious.

1 lb [455 g] baby turnips

3 cups [60 g] turnip greens or baby spinach, packed

3 Tbsp vegetable oil

Kosher salt

1 garlic clove, peeled and slightly smashed

Carrot Ginger Dressing (recipe follows)

1 Tbsp sesame seeds, toasted, for garnish

3 Tbsp roasted salted peanuts, for garnish

If your turnips have greens attached and they look fresh, remove them from the turnips, coarsely chop them, and set aside. If your turnips come loose, or the greens look wilted or unappetizing, use spinach instead. Wash the turnips thoroughly and cut them in half. If they're on the larger side, cut in quarters. In a medium bowl, toss the turnips with 2 Tbsp of the oil and 1 tsp salt.

Heat your grill to high. Place the turnips on the rack closer to one side, so you have enough room to put a skillet on the other side. Grill the turnips, covered, until they are golden, have even grill marks, and are tender when tested with a fork, 10 to 12 minutes total.

While the turnips are grilling, put the remaining 1 Tbsp of oil and the garlic in a cast-iron skillet. Place the skillet on the grill next to the turnips. Swipe the greens through the same bowl you used to season the turnips, so they get a slight coating of oil and salt. When the garlic starts to sizzle, add the greens. Cover the grill again and let the greens wilt and cook, tossing occasionally, for 3 or 4 minutes. Carefully remove the skillet from the grill (the handle will be hot!) and transfer the greens to a plate. Arrange the turnips on top, drizzle generously with the dressing, and garnish with toasted sesame seeds and peanuts. Serve immediately.

INDOOR METHOD: Preheat the broiler. Trim, oil and season the turnips as directed. On a foil-lined baking sheet, broil the turnips, tossing a few times, until they are well charred in spots and tender, 8 to 10 minutes. Cook the greens as directed with the pan on the stovetop over medium heat rather than on the grill. Proceed with the remainder of the recipe as directed.

To assemble the salad, remove the foil packet of potatoes from the grill (a metal baking sheet is a good landing spot) and carefully open. When the potatoes are cool enough to handle, cut them in halves or quarters. In a large bowl, combine the potatoes, beans, remaining 1 cup [20 g] arugula, and pesto and toss carefully so that everything is evenly coated. Scatter the pickled shallots over the top and garnish with additional chopped parsley.

INDOOR METHOD: In a large pot, bring the potatoes and enough salted water to cover by 2 inches [5 cm] to a boil. (You won't use the oil needed if you are grilling.) Lower the heat and simmer until the potatoes are tender and easily pierced with a sharp knife, about 25 minutes. Drain and let cool. Proceed with the remainder of the recipe as directed.

GRIBICHE POTATO SALAD

This potato salad has all of the flavors of the classic French sauce gribiche. There are many versions of this sauce: some are smooth like briny mayonnaise, and others have more texture. This one is less refined in a way that pairs perfectly with the hot potatoes, which soak up the flavorful oil.

3 large eggs

1½ lbs [680 g] small potatoes

⅓ cup [80 ml] plus 2 Tbsp extra-virgin olive oil

Kosher salt

1 medium shallot, finely chopped

2 Tbsp champagne or white wine vinegar, plus more if needed

¼ cup [15 g] finely chopped flat-leaf parsley

2 Tbsp finely sliced fresh chives

Zest of ½ lemon

1 Tbsp capers, drained

3 cornichons, finely chopped

2 Tbsp fresh lemon juice

1 tsp Dijon mustard

1 fennel bulb, trimmed and thinly sliced

Put the eggs in a small saucepan and cover with cold water. Bring to a boil, let boil 1 minute, and then turn off the heat. After 12 minutes, transfer the eggs to an ice bath. When the eggs are cool enough to handle, peel and dice them.

To cook the potatoes, heat the grill to medium. Fold over a very large piece of heavy-duty aluminum foil, so you have a double-layered 24-in [60-cm] square. Wash the potatoes and, with water still clinging to them, pile them on one side of your foil. You might need to lift up the edges a bit so the potatoes don't roll

away. Drizzle the potatoes with 2 Tbsp of the oil and sprinkle with salt. If using a gas grill, place the packet on the rack and flip it halfway through the grilling time. If using a charcoal grill, place the packet either in the coals or on the rack, and flip it halfway through. Cook until the potatoes are tender and a knife easily slips through them, about 35 minutes total.

While the potatoes are cooking, make the dressing. Put the shallot in a small bowl with the vinegar. Set aside. In a large bowl, combine the parsley, chives, lemon zest, capers, cornichons, lemon juice, mustard, and the remaining ⅓ cup [80 ml] oil. Now add the shallot-vinegar mixture, the fennel, and the diced eggs and stir gently.

When the potatoes are done, remove the packet from the grill (a metal baking sheet is a good landing spot) and carefully open. When the potatoes are cool enough to handle, cut them in halves or quarters, depending on the size. Add them to the bowl with the dressing and again stir gently to combine. Taste and adjust the seasoning by adding more salt or vinegar, if desired. The salad should taste bright, with strong briny flavors from the capers and cornichons.

INDOOR METHOD: Prepare the eggs as directed. In a large pot, bring the potatoes and enough salted water to cover by 2 inches [5 cm] to a boil. (You won't use the oil needed if you are grilling.) Lower the heat and simmer until the potatoes are tender and easily pierced with a sharp knife, about 25 minutes. Drain and let cool. Proceed with the remainder of the recipe as directed.

PATATAS BRAVAS FRIES

These "fries" are addictive, and even more so when served with ketchup's smoky Spanish cousin. Be sure to cook the potatoes low and slow, especially if you're using a charcoal grill.

3 plum tomatoes

¼ yellow onion

2 garlic cloves, unpeeled

1 Tbsp pimentón or other smoked paprika

1 Tbsp tomato paste

⅓ cup [80 ml] plus 3 Tbsp extra-virgin olive oil

Kosher salt

4 russet potatoes, cut into planks ½ in [12 mm] wide (like steak fries)

¼ cup [10 g] finely chopped flat-leaf parsley, for garnish

Classic Aioli and Variations (page 20, optional), for serving

Heat your grill to medium-high. Add the tomatoes, onion, and garlic, grilling until the onion is evenly charred and has softened, about 8 minutes. Grill the tomatoes until they are also evenly charred on all sides and the skin has started to blister, but before they have fallen apart, about 6 minutes total. Remove the garlic when the skin is blackened and the cloves are soft when pressed. Peel and discard the skins when cool enough to handle. Transfer the garlic, tomatoes, and onion to a blender. Add the pimentón, tomato paste, ⅓ cup [80 ml] of the oil, and a big pinch of salt and blend until smooth. Check the seasoning and transfer to a bowl; set the dipping sauce aside.

To cook the potatoes, reduce the heat to medium or let the coals cool to medium or medium-low heat. Coat the potato planks with the remaining 3 Tbsp of oil (I like to do this on a baking sheet) and sprinkle with salt. Lay the fries in a single layer on the grill and cover. Cook until both sides have grill marks and are golden and the potatoes are cooked through, 6 to 8 minutes per side.

Transfer the fries to a plate, garnish with the parsley, and serve with the tomato dipping sauce and aioli, if desired.

INDOOR METHOD: To prepare the dipping sauce, broil all of the vegetables on a foil-lined baking sheet, following the same cues for doneness as when grilling. Proceed with the recipe as directed. For the potatoes, preheat the oven to 450°F [230°C]. Oil and season the potatoes as directed. On a foil-lined baking sheet, roast the potato slices, flipping once halfway through, until they're deeply caramelized and cooked through, 30 to 40 minutes total. Proceed with the remainder of the recipe as directed.

SERVES 4

SWEET POTATO FRIES WITH TAMARIND DATE KETCHUP

The complex tanginess of the ketchup complements the smoky sweetness of the sweet potatoes.

SWEET POTATO FRIES

½ tsp kosher salt

¼ tsp ground coriander

¼ tsp chili powder

4 sweet potatoes, cut into ½- to ¾-in [12-mm to 2-cm] wedges

¼ cup [60 ml] extra-virgin olive oil

TAMARIND DATE KETCHUP

1 Tbsp tamarind paste

3 medjool dates, pitted

½ tsp kosher salt

½-in [12-mm] piece peeled fresh ginger

¼ tsp ground coriander

¼ tsp ground cumin

¼ tsp chili powder

1 cup [240 ml] Fire-Roasted Ketchup (page 23) or store-bought ketchup

TO MAKE THE SWEET POTATO FRIES: In a small bowl, stir together the salt, coriander, and chili powder. In a large bowl or on a rimmed baking sheet, toss the potatoes with the oil and then with the spice mixture.

Heat a gas grill to medium. If using a charcoal grill, let the coals cool to medium. Grill the sweet potatoes over direct heat until both sides of each wedge have taken on grill marks and some color, about 3 minutes. Once the sweet potatoes have begun to caramelize, move them to a cooler part of the grill and cover. Cook until tender, 15 to 20 minutes more, flipping them halfway through the grilling time.

TO MAKE THE TAMARIND DATE KETCHUP: Combine the tamarind, dates, salt, ginger, coriander, cumin, chili powder, ketchup, and ¼ cup [60 ml] water in a blender. Blend until smooth.

Serve the sweet potato wedges immediately with the tamarind date ketchup on the side.

INDOOR METHOD: Preheat the oven to 450°F [230°C]. Oil and season the sweet potatoes as directed. Divide the potato slices between two baking sheets (to avoid overcrowding) and roast the sweet potatoes, flipping once halfway through, until they're deeply caramelized and crisp, 20 to 30 minutes total. Proceed with the remainder of the recipe as directed.

CROSTINI WITH GRILLED OLIVE TAPENADE, CITRUS, AND GOAT CHEESE

Grilled bread could feel right at home with just about anything in this book, and any meal at all, really. Typically, crostini are baguette slices that have been brushed with oil, sprinkled with salt, and toasted until golden. Grilling the olives intensifies their flavor. You can use pretty much any olives, but I particularly like a mix of meaty, bright castelvetranos and more delicate kalamatas.

GRILLED OLIVE TAPENADE
2 cups [300 g] pitted olives
3 Tbsp extra-virgin olive oil
2 tsp finely chopped fresh thyme leaves
1 tsp finely grated orange or tangerine zest

CROSTINI
1 baguette sliced ½ in [12 mm] thick
Extra-virgin olive oil, for brushing
Kosher salt
6 oz [110 g] soft goat cheese

TO MAKE THE TAPENADE: Heat the grill to medium-high heat. Using a grill topper (or a piece of aluminum foil), cook the olives until they're charred in spots, about 8 minutes. Turn the grill to medium or let the coals cool a bit.

When the olives have cooled slightly, finely chop by hand or in a food processor. Transfer the olives to a small bowl and stir in the oil, thyme, and orange zest.

TO MAKE THE CROSTINI: Lay the baguette slices on a baking sheet. Brush them with the oil and season lightly with salt. Once the grill's temperature is down to medium, grill until the slices are golden and toasted, 1 to 2 minutes per side. Return the crostini to the baking sheet.

Spread the crostini with goat cheese and top each piece with about a teaspoon of the olive tapenade. Drizzle with any remaining oil or sprinkle additional fresh thyme, if desired.

FLATBREAD AND SUGGESTED TOPPINGS

It's no secret that bread grilled over an open flame is incredibly delicious. Plain, brushed with a bit of olive oil, and sprinkled with salt, it's a perfect vehicle for dips like the Smoky Eggplant Dip (page 28) or accompaniment to the Burst and Fresh Tomatoes with Halloumi and Basil Oil (page 42). It can also be topped with pretty much anything, from fresh cheeses to smashed avocado to grilled peaches and prosciutto. While it does work with the old standby tomato sauce and mozzarella treatment, I beg you to think of this as "flatbread topped with something," rather than "pizza" exactly, since the cheese will never get toasty and blistered, such a key part of pizza. It's not pizza's best showing, but as "flatbreads topped with something," they're extraordinary. So, that said, top away.

There are a few ways to get flatbread onto a grill. With respect to the dough, let's call the ways easy, medium, and hard. The easy method is to buy ready-made pizza dough at the grocery store. The grilling technique, described below, is the same once the dough is ready to go.

Prepare the dough according to one of the methods on the following page.

TO GRILL THE DOUGH: Pour into an 18-by-26-in [46-by-66 cm] or 9-by-13-in [23-by-33 cm] baking sheet enough olive oil to make a thin layer. (Add more oil as necessary as you grill.) Heat your grill to medium. Divide the dough (whichever you are using) into 6 to 8 balls about the size of a baseball, 2 to 3 in [5 to 7.5 cm] in diameter. Working with one ball at a time, either stretch the dough with your hands or use a rolling pin to flatten it until you have an oval about ¼ in [6 mm] thick. Working close to your grill and holding the flatbread at one edge, in one motion swipe one side of the flatbread through the oil on the baking sheet so it's completely coated, then the other side, and then land the dough on the grill. Cook for 3 to 4 minutes until the dough easily lifts up and is golden on the underside. Flip and cook for another 3 to 4 minutes until puffed and golden on both sides. Transfer to a plate. Plain flatbreads keep for 2 or 3 days. To reheat, toast in the oven, or heat briefly again on the grill.

INDOOR METHOD: Preheat the oven to 500°F [260°C]. Instead of oiling the dough itself, lightly oil a baking sheet and lay down the stretched dough. Top as desired (zucchini and corn can go on raw, precook broccoli, mushrooms, and peppers), brush any exposed crust with a bit more olive oil, and cook until the crust is golden, 15 to 18 minutes.

MEDIUM

This recipe is close to Jim Lahey's, of Sullivan Street Bakery fame. The whole-wheat flour adds nice heft to the flatbread once it's grilled, but if that's not your thing, use all white flour or experiment with different proportions.

2½ cups [350 g] whole-wheat flour
1¼ cups [175 g] all-purpose flour
2½ tsp active dry yeast (1 packet)
¾ tsp granulated sugar
2 tsp kosher salt

In a large bowl, stir together the whole-wheat flour, all-purpose flour, yeast, sugar, and salt until well combined. Make a well in the center of the flour mixture and pour 1⅓ cups [320 ml] warm water into the middle. Using a wooden spoon or rubber spatula, mix until the dough becomes too stiff to continue stirring, and then, using your hands, knead until all of the flour is incorporated and the dough comes together. It will be stiff and dry. Cover the bowl with plastic wrap and leave out at room temperature for 2 to 3 hours, until the dough has roughly doubled in size. If you're not using the dough right away, refrigerate it, covered, for up to 24 hours, or shape it into 6 balls, lightly oil them, and freeze in individual zip-top bags for several weeks.

HARDER

This dough is by no means hard, but it requires more time and attention than the other. However, the resulting flatbread is the most flavorful of the options. Additionally, you can make this bread by hand or use a mixer with a dough hook.

1 tsp honey
2½ tsp active dry yeast (1 packet)
3 cups [420 g] whole-wheat flour
3 tsp kosher salt
¾ cup [180 ml] plain Greek yogurt
1 Tbsp extra-virgin olive oil
2 to 3 cups [280 to 420 g] all-purpose flour

In a large bowl, stir together the honey, yeast, and 2 cups [480 ml] warm water with a wooden spoon, until the honey and yeast are dissolved. Add the whole-wheat flour and stir again until well combined. Let the mixture sit, uncovered, for 15 minutes.

Sprinkle the salt over the dough and then add the yogurt, olive oil, and 2 cups of all-purpose flour. Stir with a wooden spoon, mix with your hands, or use a mixer with a dough hook to work the dough for 5 to 10 minutes (5 if you're using a mixer; 10 if you're doing it by hand), until it's smooth and elastic, adding additional all-purpose flour if it starts to get sticky.

Let the dough rise, covered with plastic wrap, until doubled in size, 2 to 3 hours at room temperature or in the refrigerator overnight.

CONTINUED

TOPPINGS

The sky's the limit in terms of flatbread toppings. Here are a few things to keep in mind: cheese never gets that bronzed crust that you get from a pizza oven, so using fresh cheeses that don't rely on getting melted—like ricotta or burrata—works well, as does using hard salty ones like Parmesan or pecorino romano. Precook vegetables, such as broccoli, mushrooms, zucchini, etc., since the flatbread's time on the grill is short. Sauces, such as tomato sauce, work but should be used sparingly, to prevent crust sogginess. Sauces added after the flatbread is cooked, such as pesto, are dynamite. To top flatbreads, either add the toppings once the dough is off the grill, or if you do need to melt or heat toppings through, add them just after flipping the dough.

TOPPING SUGGESTIONS

- **RICOTTA, CHARRED ASPARAGUS, AND PROSCIUTTO:** Toss asparagus with oil and salt and grill alongside the flatbread. When the flatbread is off the grill, spread a thin layer of ricotta over the whole round, add full spears of asparagus or chop into bite-size pieces, and lay slices of prosciutto over the top. Finish with lemon zest, flaky salt, and freshly ground black pepper.

- **GRILLED ZUCCHINI, FRESH CORN, FETA, AND CLASSIC BASIL PESTO (PAGE 19):** Thinly slice zucchini lengthwise; brush both sides of each slice with olive oil and sprinkle with salt. Grill alongside the flatbread. Cut the kernels off of one or two ears of corn. When the flatbread comes off the grill, spread the pesto over all, lay the zucchini slices on top, scatter the corn over, and add crumbled feta cheese.

- **BURRATA WITH CHARRED BROCCOLI AND GRILLED MUSHROOMS:** Toss bite-size broccoli florets and coarsely chopped mushrooms with olive oil and salt. Grill on a grill topper until charred and crisp. When the flatbread comes off the grill, add the burrata, coarsely torn, along with the vegetables. Garnish with a drizzle of olive oil, flaky salt, and finely chopped fresh parsley or thyme.

- **GRILLED PEACHES, PARMESAN, AND ARUGULA:** Cut peaches in half and remove and discard the pits. Rub the cut sides with olive oil and season with salt. Grill, cut-side down, until the fruit is caramelized and juicy, about 5 minutes. Top the flatbread with sliced peaches, plenty of Parmesan cheese peeled with a vegetable peeler, and arugula dressed with Lemon Vinaigrette (page 14).

- **GOAT CHEESE AND GRILLED PEPPERS:** Grill peppers as for Romesco Sauce (page 50). Spread the flatbread with goat cheese just after flipping so it starts to warm. Top with the peppers and a sprinkling of dried or fresh oregano and a drizzle of balsamic vinegar.

- **AVOCADO AND PICKLED SHALLOTS:** When the flatbread comes off the grill, smash half an avocado on the round, and top with flaky salt, freshly ground pepper, and Pickled Shallots (page 30).

ACKNOWLEDGMENTS

Thank you to all of my eaters, editors, recipe testers, and champions. Most of all, thanks to Scott, who did all of those things and more—while I was working on this book and, well, always. Thank you.

Thank you to the rest of my family—Mom and Dad, Zach and Lexi, Marshall and Heather, Bob and Barbara, Emily and Tom—for their love and support. And thank you especially for giving the gazpacho a spin on a rainy winter day, letting me turn your kitchens into my office, buying bottles of pomegranate molasses and jars of tamarind paste that you may never use again (but I hope you will!), and consuming lots and lots of vegetables.

A special thanks, also, to all of the others who tested recipes for me in New York, Philadelphia, San Francisco, Los Angeles, Minneapolis, Duxbury, Larchmont, and elsewhere. Your notes were invaluable.

Thank you to our babysitters for keeping Sam away from the grill over and over again and for keeping him happy and safe so that I could focus on this book.

Thank you, too, to the cooks at Delfina, who trained me better than any school ever could have and gave me the confidence to get here. I learned so much from you.

A profound thanks to Erin Kunkel, Lillian Kang, and their teams for their brilliant food styling and photography.

Lastly, thank you to my editor, Sarah Billingsley, and the team at Chronicle Books for making this book real.

INDEX